LEARN ACCOUNTING FAST!

Concepts and Practice

John J. Cousins

BizB Press

New York London

First published by BizB Press 2016

ISBN 978-1534614871

About the Author

John Cousins is an independent business advisor. He helps people explore opportunities so they make more money, get more done, and have more fun running their businesses. Before creating MBA-ASAP.com, he worked for ABC Television, launched seven startups, took two companies public, and was a public company CFO and CEO for 15 years. John has his MBA from Wharton and undergrad degrees from Boston University and MIT. He lives in the high desert in New Mexico.

Dedicated to my Mom

Who said to me: "If your outflow is more than
your income then your upkeep is your downfall"
A perfectly succinct summary of accounting
theory and management practice.

Contents

Preface

This book draws on a number of my academic and professional experiences. I have founded and ran a number of companies and I have been CFO and CEO of publicly traded companies for almost twenty years. More recently, I have been teaching college and graduate level accounting courses. The cumulative experience of this life trajectory of studying, working, and teaching has alerted me to the fact that there are simply no quick overview field guides to Accounting. I decided to address this knowledge gap. This slim volume fills the gap on essential accounting knowledge and skills sets. It is what you need to know in order to get going and become successful. This book is intended to be used as a quick and practical guide and as a supplement to more detailed accounting textbooks.

Introduction

"A successful book is not made of what is in it, but of what is left out of it."

Mark Twain

This is an overview of both the practical aspects and practice of Accounting. Intentionally kept short, it is intended to give you the basic information you need to handle accounting tasks and to manage accountants and bookkeepers. In order to practice accounting and manage accountants and accounting tasks you first must have a conceptual understanding of what accounting is trying to achieve. When you understand what the ends are, the means make a lot more sense. This book will provide you with the conceptual underpinnings of accounting and a context of its basic goals in simple, direct, clear language. It will also present you with an idea of the various specialties and jobs in the professional field of accounting and describe what kind of proficiency and responsibility they require.

This book is written for business oriented people and aspiring entrepreneurs who need to understand and use accounting in this new and rapidly evolving economy in order to get things done. My goal is to lead you up the steep part of the learning curve quickly and efficiently so you can begin the practice of accounting. Accounting is called a "practice" because you get good at it by doing it.

I want to first convey a practical overview ASAP and second fill in details as they come up and allow you to use them as needed. This approach can be called Just In Time knowledge as opposed to Just In Case learning. Once you are up and running, you will continue learning while you are doing; learn while you earn. At that point the concepts will really begin to stick and make sense. This information can be used as a reference tool that allows you to refer back to specific sections and cement your new knowledge.

I provide the basics in just enough detail to be comprehensive and useable. To get started you don't need total knowledge, just enough to get going and start learning by doing. The Pareto principle or the 80–20 rule, states that roughly 80% of the effects come from 20% of the causes. This volume, as all the books in the MBA ASAP series, follows this rule by focusing on the powerful 20% information.

Learning and understanding Accounting can seem initially intimidating because of all the specialized terminology. This volume seeks to familiarize you with the names, buzz words, and acronyms in business and accounting. These terms can be a barrier to further reading and study if you are not familiar with them but they are not difficult to understand and you don't have to memorize them. There is a Glossary of Terms at the end of the book. Refer to the Glossary as you come across new terminology (just in time knowledge) and as needed. This way you will soon build a working knowledge of these terms and concepts. Use the Glossary in your daily life as you read the business press and watch television business news.

You can benefit from this overview as a primer before you take a college accounting course, or as a refresher if you took one long ago. It is also a good reference volume. In a large company you can work in accounting for a long time and still not have a good idea of how it all fits together. If you have been a bookkeeper or have worked in one particular area of accounting like Accounts Receivable, this book will give you an expanded view of the entire accounting process. This knowledge can help you perform you current job better and open new opportunities for you.

Author's Note

I have two experiences to share with you that shaped my earliest and formative encounters with accounting. First, my girlfriend in college was a wonderful woman and her father was an accomplished businessman who owned and ran a company with factories in the Northeast and the Southwest. At the time I had worked numerous jobs but really had very little idea of how business in general was conducted and operated. My worldview was limited and I just did what the boss said. I had stars in my eyes and was extremely idealistic, but I had a vague unformed interest in business activities as a practical route to accomplishing grand projects. And I had an interest in money and how it was made. I remember asking him what I should first and foremost study to learn about business. Without a moment's hesitation he said: "accounting, it's the basis of all business activities." He went on to tell me that the numbers and records were the foundation of his business. At the time, it seemed disappointingly too prosaic of an answer. I was looking for some secret tip that would unveil the easy way to become a millionaire. It took me almost ten more years to begin studying accounting but his advice has stuck with me to this day.

My second seminal experience came as a jolt. I started studying accounting by jumping in the deep end of the pool. It was in my first semester of my MBA program. I had had no business courses as an undergraduate. After college I had a great career working as an electronic engineer but had no general business experience in my career to that point. I wanted an MBA to fill that knowledge gap.

So here I was sitting high up in a seminar-style amphitheater for Accounting 101 and the professor launched into the details of accounting: T accounts and debits and credits. I walked out of that lecture hall in a daze, confused by the maze of unfamiliar jargon and concepts. Accounting is not an intuitive subject.

Compared to many of my classmates I was ill equipped for the accelerated pace of study that began by taking for granted a base level of business knowledge. I had to scramble to catch up. I spent a lot of time with the book and teaching assistants and slowly got up to some sort of speed but it was hard going. And I could have been spared the anxiety had I been prepared a bit in advance with a primer like this. I still have my textbook from that class: 800 pages! I never forgot that experience.

Historical Perspective

I have added some back-story sections when they seemed relevant in order to provide a context of how these different accounting practices, disciplines and conventions arose. How we got to here and now. Conventions arise over time usually as a way to streamline or simplify workflow or address problems.

Historical accounts are provided to give you a sense of the logic of accounting practices and rules. Accounting didn't just happen or burst forth fully formed. Accounting has evolved as a rational way of keeping a record of transactions and creating a clear presentation of those records.

The industrial world is based on a lineage of technical innovations, and creative practices starting in the mid 1700s. Business practices have co-developed over the past 300 years. It started with the first Industrial Revolution and has moved through progressive inventions to our current information age. Economics evolved as a response to the emerging business world as a way of comprehending and explaining these radically new developments and their implications. The seminal text of Economics, Adam Smith's "The Wealth of Nations" was published in 1776.

Accounting is older than economics. Double entry bookkeeping is an innovation dating to the beginning of the Renaissance in the late 1400s and was a world changing innovation. Accounting practice provided a way to keep track of trade dealings and helped create vast wealth for the newly minted banking families of Florence. In fact, accounting allowed these families to prosper and create the wealth that fueled the Renaissance. As a form intellectual property, accounting is one of the most important innovations in the history of humankind.

Ready, Fire, Aim

Accounting can be intimidating. Don't wait to start actualizing your abilities. Take action, see what happens, and modify as you go along. Use this book to help you steer the course. This book will help you get it right the first time. And never underestimate the value of getting it right the first time. And don't worry about making mistakes. You can correct them quickly and they are part of the fast track to learning and expertise.

Computers have revolutionized accounting and have made the practice easier and more accurate in many ways. Spreadsheets such as Excel and accounting software like Quickbooks make our lives as accountants less error prone and radically reduce the drudgery associated with entering and adding long columns of numbers. Take it from me: It is a good time to be learning this subject.

Being an effective accountant means being able to communicate and be decisive. You must be able to communicate the work tasks internal to the company in order to record transactions and generate reports. You will need to make determinations and decisions about what level of detail is adequate for effective reporting. You need a clear understanding of who your audience is and what information they need. Your audience may include bankers, lawyers, investors, and regulators, as well as bosses and board members. There are sections that will discuss these parties and what their needs and interests are.

Accounting Basics

Let's dive into the underlying structure of business: the numbers. You need to know the basics of accounting and have a proper accounting system in place in order to run a business. It is the fundamental way that you keep track of *how* your business is doing and *what* you are doing. It is the most telling and intimate record of a business.

Learning accounting and understanding how to read financial statements can seem daunting and complicated. Yet you already have a finely calibrated sense of accounting from your daily life: it's all about money, ain't a dang thing funny... You have implicitly learned and understand the fundamentals of accounting from your experience of getting and spending. This knowledge is what you can always use as your touchstone. Every day you balance your checkbook, stretch your paycheck, pay your bills, manage your credit cards and car loan and mortgage and rent. You are running a pretty complicated enterprise! Though it may sometimes seem like it, accounting is not an arcane exercise; it is a foundational and practical part of everyday life.

Accounting needs to make sense and be direct and clear. It is the way to record all the transactions of a business and communicate them to others not intimately involved in the particulars of that business. So we need to keep it simple and direct. Keep Occam 's Razor in mind, which is the principle that the simplest solution is always the best and try to eliminate unnecessary elements.

There are two basic parts to accounting knowledge: bookkeeping and financial statements. Bookkeeping is how you enter business transaction information into your accounting system and how you track these entries. Financial statements are the reports that organize the transactional information of bookkeeping in standardized forms so an interested party can quickly grasp the financial position and performance of the enterprise. You will learn how to read **financial statements** and how **bookkeeping** entries are made, revised, and checked.

Prior to the 1980s when personal computers revolutionized accounting with software programs and spreadsheets, accounting and bookkeeping required a relatively high level of expertise, experience, and concentration. Systems had to be essentially created from scratch and each number and account was generated, entered, and written by hand on ledger sheets. You really had to know your **debits** from your **credits** and be the calculator. Now computer systems assist in creating the structure and guide the process of making entries. This makes accounting practice much more accessible and less cumbersome.

The twentieth century saw helpful innovations in accounting before computers. Adding machines and then hand held calculators were huge helps in relieving the burden of adding and subtracting columns of numbers and in reducing errors. You can imagine how tedious and mind-numbing accounting must have been before that. Poor Bob Cratchet.

In the past several decades the practice of accounting has been transformed with spreadsheets and accounting software. You are so lucky to be learning and becoming an accounting user now! You can now add and subtract and manipulate columns of numbers in spreadsheets and save them as a handy record of your work. Accounting software such as QuickBooks is easy to set up and use, and gives you prompts for how to input numbers and helps check for errors. We can also import and export between spreadsheets and accounting software and word processors to generate reports. These innovations have removed some of the biggest barriers to starting a business and running it professionally. Lucky us!

Bifurcating Accounting

Accounting tracks the monetary aspects of a business operation; where the money comes from and where it goes.

To paraphrase the humorist and actor Robert Benchley: "there are two kinds of people: those who divide things into two groups, and those who don't" To get a grasp of accounting let's break the field into two groups: **Bookkeeping** and **Financial Statements**.

Bookkeeping is the process of recording each and every transaction that takes place within a business: every check that is cut, every invoice received and entered, all the money that comes in as **Revenues** and all the money that goes out as **Expenses**; and all the **assets** and

liabilities. It is a record of all purchases, sales, receipts and payments. These business transactions occur on a daily basis and must be properly recorded in "**the books**". The books is a slang term referring to the **General Ledger** and the various journals that are kept by a business. The general ledger is a list of all the accounts grouped by the types of transactions.

Financial Statements are the reports generated of the aggregation of the bookkeeping activity. There are three main financial statements: **Balance Sheet, Income Statement,** and **Cash Flow Statement.** The two to focus on initially are the Balance Sheet and Income Statement.

Cash

The lifeblood of business is cash and keeping track of your cash position is an absolute priority. Things come to a grinding halt when the bank accounts are empty. You need cash to pay bills, purchase supplies, pay salaries (people become ornery if they don't get paid), and keep the lights on. Your accounting system keeps track of how much money is coming in (revenues) and how much is going out (expenses); how much cash you have is what is left over.

Budgets

How much cash you have on hand is the measure of how much business activity you can perform in the foresecable future. Based on your budget, you can estimate how long you can operate with a certain amount of cash in the bank. How much cash you need to spend each month for your proposed operations is called you **"burn rate."** For operating businesses the burn rate is extremely important, as is the forecasting of when revenues will be received to replenish the coffers. If you are in a pre-revenue start up phase of developing a business, the conservation and disciplined use of cash is paramount. The budget is your plan of cash use.

The amount of cash you have, divided by your burn rate is called your **"runway"**. It is a flight metaphor related to how much time you have before you need to "take off," i.e. begin replenishing cash with either revenues or a round of funding. This metric is also called your horizon to revenues.

Revenues from sales increase the cash position and fund future activity. For Start-up enterprises, the amount of cash raised is equivalent to how much development activity you can perform before you will need to achieve revenues and sales or go out and do another round of fund raising. The "**runway**" represents how long the enterprise can operate, based on the budget (and disciplined execution and adherence to that budget), before things come to a grinding halt or more money is raised. Cash is your main resource. You cannot be effective without it. A slang term for thinking of cash in this way is called "dry powder," an old fashioned gun powder analogy.

Each month it is good operating and managerial practice to compare your actual accounting results to your previously prepared budget. When you compare Actuals to Budget you are looking for variances: differences between them. These are the numbers that you need to understand. Why were you over or under budget? Was it a onetime unforeseen event or a recurring expense that you overlooked in the budgeting process? This kind of analysis forces you to have detailed answers to these questions.

If you are over budget it better be for a very good reason like it accelerated timetables or expanded opportunities. Caveat: expanding opportunities can be seductive and not necessarily productive. What seem to be expanded opportunities can dilute efforts and actually reduce chances of success. You can't successfully chase all the possibilities that present themselves. Part of disciplined execution and management is focusing on the specific goals and eliminating or reducing distractions; even if they seem attractive. Remember the Sirens from the Odyssey...

Keeping Track

Your computer-based accounting system helps keep track of all of these considerations so you can report and operate your business in an organized and planned manner. In comparing actuals to budget you may need to export or import data between your accounting system and a spreadsheet program. The current versions of software have easy functions to accommodate import and export sharing between programs.

Now we will discuss bookkeeping and the basic process of making journal entries, posting them, and creating financial statements from that information.

Bookkeeping

Preparing and maintaining the accounting books is the task of bookkeeping and bookkeepers. Bookkeeping creates of a record of every transaction that a business makes. As you get money in and pay bills and have money going out, every transaction gets recorded in the books. Records are maintained of every transaction: all receipts, invoices, check stubs, purchase orders and packing slips are kept in orderly files related to each time period (months, years), by transaction type, vendor, or account. Bookkeeping is about recording transactions as journal entries of debits and credits and posting them to the general ledger.

Setting Up the Books

When we talk of the "books" what we refer to is the group of all the accounts of the transactions of an enterprise. This list or group makes up the general ledger. The general ledger is the collection of all asset, liability, equity, revenue and expense accounts. Transactions are grouped together in some related way as accounts and accounts are grouped and categorized into the General Ledger ("GL"). Transactions are usually related by vendor, customer or type of transaction. For example, all of your office rent payments would be grouped in an account called "Landlord" or "Office Rent" or something similar. Your sales income might be grouped by customer, or simply in a general "sales revenue" account; all of your electric bills and payments would be recorded in an account set up for the utility company. This list of accounts and vendors is the basic organizing principle of your accounting system. When you initially start an accounting system for a company you create a **chart of accounts** that classifies different groupings of business transactions. The chart of accounts is a listing of all accounts used in the **general ledger** of an organization. The chart of accounts simply a laundry list of all the accounts. Usually when you begin working for an existing company the chart of accounts already exists and as new vendors occur, a new account is added. The vendor list shows information about the people or companies from whom you buy goods and services, including banks and tax agencies.

You need to be familiar with this organizing structure conceptually, but remember; rarely are you called on to set up a **chart of accounts** and **vendor list** from scratch. In most accounting situations you will be introduced to an already set up and functioning system. If you are in a position of starting a company you will lack internal supporting resources. At some point early on you can hire an experienced accountant as a consultant to help set up your system, including the chart of accounts and vendor list, and coach you and review your initial entries. If you are involved in a start up or small company, having a pro review your books and processes on a regular basis like once a month or quarter is a good idea. Another set of eyes is always helpful. Be honest about the level of your abilities but don't be intimidated. After reading this book you know enough of what you need to identify, interview and hire an accounting consultant or a staff accountant when the time comes.

The Accounting Cycle

The accounting cycle refers to the sequence of activities that occur in the accounting process from the occurrence of a transaction though the generating financial statements.

- Recognition of the event as a transaction and identify and file the source document: receipt, bill, check, invoice etc.

- Analysis of the transaction to determine which accounts are affected and in which direction (debit or credit)
- **Journal Entries**: the transaction is recorded in the journal as a debit and a credit. (a transaction can have more than one debit or credit, but the debits must equal the credits so that they balance)
- Post to the Ledger: the journal entries are transferred to the appropriate **T-accounts** in the **general ledger**
- **Trial Balance**: an unadjusted trial balance is generated and calculated to verify that the sum of the debits is equal to the sum of the credits. This is a point in the process where some iterative work may have to be done to locate any errors if and when the debits and credits don't initially balance.
- **Adjusting Entries**: are made of accrued and deferred items (the ones from the operations section of the cash flow statement)

- Adjusted Trial Balance: a new trial balance is calculated after making the adjusting entries
- Financial Statements: prepare the financial statement from the adjusted trial balance
- Closing Entries: transfer the temporary accounts such as revenues and expenses to owner's equity.
- After-closing Trial Balance: prepare a post-closing trial balance in order to check all the accounts

The good news is that your accounting software will perform these tasks for you. You only need to enter the transaction. However, you need to be familiar with the process so you can quickly troubleshoot any mistakes if the balances between debits and credits don't match. You will make lots of these mistakes but there is no need to be concerned. Even very experienced accountants make errors. The key is to realize it and quickly locate them and fix them. The accounting cycle process provides the step-by-step methodology and helps us error-prone humans.

The accounting cycle is a methodical set of steps that help ensure the accuracy and conformity of financial statements. You follow these steps like a recipe. Computerized accounting systems have helped to greatly reduce entry and mathematical errors in the accounting process, and the uniform and rigorous process of the accounting cycle also helps reduce mistakes and maintain consistency. Accounting is a detail-oriented activity. The accounting cycle steps are a checklist that helps promote accuracy. The deity is in the details.

Bookkeeping Flow

There is a process flow to how business transactions are entered and recorded into the accounting books. The Accounting Cycle section above details the steps of the flow. The following section provides more details about the steps in the bookkeeping parts of the cycle.

Transactions are initiated through a form of documented request: an invoice, or a bill, or a contract. These are entered as obligations: a payable, or receivable, or as a cash disbursement, or revenues. In other words, either you receive money (**revenue** or **sales**), or pay money (**expenses**), or you are owed money (**account receivable**), or you are obligated to pay money (**account payable**).

Each transaction is entered as a **Journal Entry**. Each journal entry impacts two accounts by essentially reducing one account and increasing another. This is called **double entry** bookkeeping. The two entries offset each other as a **debit** and a **credit**. A transaction can impact more than just two accounts. In this case there will be debits and credits to multiple accounts. But the sum total of the debits must equal the sum total of the credits. An example would be paying for a piece of equipment partially with cash and partly with a loan; this would impact three accounts and the total of the cash and loan would equal the price of the equipment.

All journal entries are posted to the general ledger. In a specific period like a month, or quarter, or year, they aggregate up to form the basis of the financial statements. This journal entry process is the start and the essence of bookkeeping and since financial statements are the summation of all the bookkeeping entries, it is the foundation of the entire accounting process.

Debits and Credits

Debit and **credit** are the two most basic accounting terms to become familiar with. They represent the fundamental concept of bookkeeping. However, the practice of double entry bookkeeping and the application of debits and credits to accounts is not intuitive and will take some time to get used to. With that in mind, let's discuss the concepts more.

In accounting, there are two sides to every transaction and they are called **debit** and **credit**. Each journal entry affects at least two accounts; it can affect a group of debits and a group of credits but they must equal each other. This is a concept that may take a while to get your head around and get used to. But you will. Think of a situation where you lend someone $10. Like Shakespeare said, there are two sides to this IOU type transaction: the borrower and the lender. You record that you expect the money back (**asset**) and the other party records that they expect to pay it back (**liability**). All transactions are two sided like this example: one account is enhanced and one account is depleted. Or think of a deli counter transaction: you get a sandwich and the deli gets money. But each side records two entries. From the deli side, they get money, which increases their revenue, and they give up a sandwich, which depletes their inventory. From your side, you get a delicious sandwich which is an asset (albeit temporary), and you give up money, which depletes your bank account. Each side records a double entry transaction. Each sides transaction entry is a mirror image of the other: what you gain, they give up, and vice versa. Accounting is a zero sum endeavor.

Debit and Credit can be tricky concepts to initially understand. Here is an another attempt at a simple explanation. A Debit increases the resources of the enterprise and a Credit reduces the resources. So with Asset accounts, ones that are resources, a Debit will increase the account. With a Liability account, ones that are obligations of the enterprise, a Debit will decrease that account; because the decrease of a liability, like say a loan, means in essence to increase the resources of the company. Think of this as if you pay off a credit card, you have increased your resources by no longer carrying that debt obligation (and at the same time you save a ton of interest payments!)

Credits are the mirror image opposite. When you pay a bill, you credit cash (an asset account) because you have reduced the amount of cash you have. If you take out a loan, you credit the loan account (a liability account) because you have increased an obligation of the company.

You will probably have to refer back to this concept of debits and credits several times. Just acknowledge that this concept may be challenging and don't become frustrated, it will become clear with use.

Here is a short cheat sheet to help.

Cheat Sheet for Debits and Credits

Asset accounts have **debit** balances.

- Debits **increase** Asset accounts.
- Credits **decrease** Asset accounts.

Liability accounts have **credit** balances.

- Credits **increase** Liability Accounts.
- Debits **decrease** Liability Accounts.

Equity accounts have **credit** balances.

- Credits **increase** Equity Accounts.
- Debits **decrease** Equity Accounts.

Income accounts have **credit** balances.

- Credits **increase** Income Accounts.
- Debits **decrease** Income Accounts.

Cost of Goods Sold accounts
have **debit** balances.

- Debits **increase** Cost of Goods Sold accounts.
- Credits **decrease** Cost of Goods Sold accounts.

Expense accounts have **debit** balances.

- Debits **increase** Expense accounts.
- Credits **decrease** Expense accounts.

History of Double Entry Accounting

The concept of debits and credits may seem mundane; if not obvious, but in fact double entry bookkeeping is one of the great innovations in the history of civilization. Its invention and adoption represents one of the great inflection points in history.

The first recorded description of double entry bookkeeping was in 1458 in a work titled: ***Book on the Art of Trade***. The author's name was Benedikt Kotruljević, who was born in Ragusa or what is now known as Dubrovnik in 1416. It is considered a great intellectual breakthrough and he is famous in Dubrovnik. Bookkeeping in this manner enabled merchants, entrepreneurs and their investors to keep track of every penny they received or spent.

The invention of double entry bookkeeping is usually attributed to being invented in Milan by Luca Pacioli. Luca wrote the *Summa de Arithmetica, Geometria,*

Proportioni et Proportionalita in 1494 and was living with Leonardo da Vinci as his math teacher at the time.

The idea was first implemented in a functional way by the Medici's and other banking families of Florence in the late 1400s. This concept was their trade secret that allowed Florence to become a very rich and powerful city-state conducting wide ranging international trade. It gave the city the financial resources to become the center and engine of the Renaissance, change the course of history, and start humanity on the course of becoming modern; of becoming us.

Double entry bookkeeping represents an ingenious work-around for a society that had yet to discover the powerful number zero. It is strange for us to imagine the idea of zero as being a breakthrough innovation. The concept of Zero came to the West through Persia and the Ottomans via India.   The two countervailing numbers that cancel each other out in double entry bookkeeping were a way to show the impact of a transaction on two parties or on assets and liabilities whose net effect is equal to zero.

The history of accounting is tied to the history of trade and thus the history of human progress. Accounting is an extremely important and influential innovation. Keep this legacy in mind as you study and learn it.

Accrual vs. Cash Accounting

Most accounting is done on an **accrual** basis as opposed to a cash basis. Accrual means that transactions are recorded when they occur, not when cash is received or dispersed. Conversely, cash basis accounting calls for the recognition of an expense when the cash goes out the door, regardless of when the expense was actually incurred; and recognition of revenue only when cash is received, not taking into account when the corresponding sale was actually consummated. Although cash basis accounting may seem logical at first glance, it leads to confusions in recording and reporting the operations of the business.

Accrual accounting provides you with a more accurate picture of the business activities. Here is an example of accrual accounting: your business has sold a product and the customer has 60 days to pay; the transaction is booked as a receivable so it is recorded that revenue was generated at that time but cash wasn't collected; when the cash is collected, the receivable is cleared out (credit) and cash is recorded (debit). On one side of the equation, the customer received the product and a transaction clearly has occurred. On the other side, the cash has not been collected for the sale. The receivable records the obligation. This completes both sides of the transaction with a debit and credit recording.

If you recorded this transaction on a cash basis you would record the cost of the sale two months before you recorded the receipt of the cash, so you would have more expenses one month and more revenues in another. That is not an accurate picture of what has occurred. Take a look at the Khan Academy videos (KhanAcademy.org) on accrual vs. cash accounting. Sal does a great job of explaining it by running through some comparison examples.

Accrual accounting operates on the principal of matching expenses and revenues in the same period for a given transaction. There are basically two kinds of accounts that are created to record accrual type activities:

- **Accounts Receivable** (AR) which deals with money that is owed to you but not yet received
- **Accounts Payable** (AP) which deals with bills that have been received and recorded but not yet paid

Accrual accounting is based on the **matching principle**. The **matching principle** states that expenses should be recorded during the period in which they are incurred, regardless of when the transfer of cash occurs. If cash has not yet been collected related to a sale then the expense should be matched to an **Accounts Receivable**. If a bill is acknowledged as something to be paid but the check has not yet been cut, then the liability should be entered as an Accounts Payable.

A transaction is usually determined to have occurred based on this cause and effect relationship. If no cause-

and-effect relationship exists such as a sale or purchase, costs are recognized as expenses in the accounting period they occurred.

Prepaid expenses are not recognized as expenses in the period that you pay them. They represent an asset that will be used over time. Prepaid expenses provide future benefits. Prepaid expenses are booked as assets until they are used and the benefit is received. At this point, that used or spent portion is recognized as an expense. As a prepaid expense is used up, an **adjusting entry** is made to update the reduced value of the asset. In the case of prepaid rent, the cost of rent for the period would be deducted from the Prepaid Rent account.

The matching principle and accrual accounting allow for a more objective and accurate analysis of profitability. By recognizing costs in the period they are incurred, a business can see how much money was spent to generate revenue, reducing "noise" from timing mismatches between when costs are incurred and when revenue is realized.

Payroll

Payroll is an accounting function that administers paying all employees, calculating the appropriate withholdings for taxes, and processes all the checks or direct deposits. Payroll is performed on a regular repeating schedule. Typical schedules are: weekly, every two weeks, or on the first and fifteenth of the month. The first and 15th is a good schedule as it smoothes out the differences in the amount of days in each month. An employee receives two checks per month and can better plan their monthly budget and expenses. Also it ends on the last day of the year which is important for keeping annual payroll accounting less complicated. Payroll is paid for work completed; employees are paid for the prior period's work.

There are a number of withholding deductions that are made from gross payroll. These withholding deductions include: Federal and state taxes, Social Security, workers comp, and Unemployment. They are calculated on an individual basis per employee. QuickBooks and other accounting software provide schedules for calculating these. New schedule come out annually and need to be updated as tax rates and other details may change. Accounting software also provides for the printing of checks and including the reporting the withholding amounts and net pay. Special checks are ordered for the printer and usually include, besides the check number, two copies of detail portion: one for the employee and one for your files.

There are also payroll services that outsource the entire payroll process. The number of employees, the size of the payroll, and your in-house resources are determining factors of whether to employ a payroll service or do it in-house. You may decide to outsource at first and bring it in-house as you grow, or vice versa. It is something to routinely consider as your company grows. An added advantage of payroll services consists in the fact of having more controls and procedures in place when cutting large numbers of checks, and also offsets some liabilities if mistakes are made.

Fraud Prevention

Controls and Procedures

There are many points in the accounting cycle that are vulnerable to fraud. Bookkeepers and accountants have big responsibilities. As such we need a solid sense of business ethics. We handle the day-to-day money operations and need to be scrupulously honest and not tempted to steal. A company is prey to fraud and stealing from the personnel who report the transactions, maintain the books, and cut the checks. And the people who are responsible for this work are prey to rationalizing bad behavior. A glance at the business news any day provides many examples of these type bad actors.

From a business operator's perspective we need to be aware of these temptations and institute controls and procedures to protect against them. These concerns are also extremely important if you are lucky enough to be a successful performer or artist. There are a lot of tragic stories of musicians and other artists being ripped off by their accountants and managers or a combination of the two. It is crucial to have a knowledge of accounting in order to review your books with your accountant and manager and scrutinize the methods being used.

Separating the duties associated with managing and reporting the money that comes in and goes out of a business is extremely important in order to protect against fraud. This process is codified and formalized in the Controls and Procedures document. It is also important to have mechanisms in place to quickly detect any unusual transactions and track down their origins. This kind of scrutiny will aid in preventing anyone tempted to defraud you. The perception of easy money and the prospect of getting it can easily lead to a distorted perception of reality.

Documented procedures need to be developed *and followed* relating to:

- who opens the mail,
- who records the transactions,
- who reviews and authorizes payments
- who prepares the checks to pay bills
- who reviews and signs the checks,

- who reconciles the accounts,
- who reviews the books.

These functions need to be separated and records reviewed on a regular basis in order to help prevent fraud. You may not be able to eliminate the possibility of fraud but you can take steps to create an environment in which it is difficult to perpetrate it.

Good accounting systems prevent fraud

Your accounting system also provides a record of every transaction and, when managed properly, helps insure against fraud, theft, and "leakage". Review of financial statements is an important part of identifying and preventing fraud. We have all heard horror stories of entertainers and other victims who were taken advantage of by unscrupulous managers and accountants. Learning accounting and how to read and assess accounting records or "books" through financial statement review will help protect you and your assets against such a fate. Just an aside: The incredible longevity and success of the Rolling Stones is due in no small part to their business savvy (and incredible musical and songwriting talent!) Mick Jagger is a graduate of the London School of Economics. Word to the wise…

Computer- Based Accounting Systems

We are now going to discuss accounting software. There is absolutely no reason to do accounting manually these days. Software packages are inexpensive and have major advantages such as speed and accuracy of operation, record storage and, the ability to see the real-time state of the company's financial position.

There are many different software packages to handle business accounting. I recommend QuickBooks as the accounting software to start. QuickBooks is by Intuit who also owns TurboTax. It has become the standard accounting software for small businesses because it has a huge installed base of experienced users. There are many consultants and small business accountants that can help you set it up and get running. The company provides very good instructional tutorials and support. And there is also tons of instructional information on YouTube and other sites such as Lynda.com. In most cases you can set it up and operate it yourself. You can learn basic QuickBooks in a matter of hours with these online resources and tutorials. Find an experienced user and ask a few questions if you run into an impasse. There is a cloud based version that is attractive because it is less expensive as an entry option and is convenient from an IT standpoint. You don't have to load and install the program on your computer, just set up an account and you are ready to go. There are many alternative systems to QuickBooks that you can explore online. But taking the easy alternative means one less thing to think about.

Users of Accounting Information

Management needs to know how the overall company is performing or how their division is doing. Managers may need feedback ASAP on how a new marketing campaign or pricing strategy is working. When and how transactions are booked is very important to users of accounting information. Users need timely information about how the business is doing in order to make decisions.

Besides the internal interests of management, there are external users of accounting information such as:

- Bankers who are interested in your credit worthiness and ability to repay loans,
- Vendors who are interested in your ability to pay and your credit worthiness,
- Investors who want to know whether to invest or how their investment is performing,
- Stock Analysts who research companies and opine on whether or not they are good investments for their clients,
- Potential customers, especially of big ticket items or services, who want to know that the company is sound and will be around to offer support and spare parts, and
- Taxing authorities who want to know how much money the business has made or lost.

Reporting the results of business activity on an accrual basis is important to these parties that have a stake in the company's performance and health. Accrual provides a much more accurate picture of the operations to those who are not intimately involved in the day-to-day operations but need to know the operational details.

The way this kind of reporting of the accounting information is prepared, organized, and conveyed is in Financial Statements.

Financial Statements

Financial statements are reports. They are the formats in which accounting information is organized so *users* of financial information have a consistent, quick, and thorough means of reading and understanding what is going on in the business. There are two basic financial statements: the **Balance Sheet** and the **Income Statement**.

Interested parties need to understand the financial and accounting activities of a business. The Balance Sheet and Income Statement are a formal record of the financial activities of a business, presented in a structured manner and in a form easy to understand.

Financial Statements provide a high level view of accounting and a summary of how a business is performing. They provide a quick picture that can be easily compared across businesses and industries. Understanding how to read and analyze a Balance Sheet and Income Statement is a great place to start understanding accounting and finance. It is the end-point of bookkeeping; it's the goal. When you know where you are going and who the audience is, it is easier to make good bookkeeping decisions. When you understand the liquidity, solvency and capital structure of a company you can make good financing and investment decisions.

Financial Statements are the tools and information required to quickly analyze and assess the relative health of a business. A basic understanding of financial statements also provides the high level perspective on the goals of the bookkeeping work and entries. The daily operations of a business are measured in the money that comes in as revenues, the money that goes out as expenses, and the money that is retained as profit. It's all about the money.

The report that measures these daily operations, of money in and money out over a period of time, is the Income Statement.

Income Statement

The Income Statement can be summarized as: Revenues less Expenses equals Net Income. The term Net Income simply means Income (Revenues) net (less) of Expenses. Net Income is also called Profit or Earnings. You understand this concept intuitively. We always strive to sell things for more than they cost us to make or purchase. When you buy a house you hope that it will appreciate in value so you can sell it in the future for more than you paid for it. In order to have a sustainable business model in the long run, the same logic applies.

Think of the Income Statement in relation to your monthly personal finances. You have your monthly revenues: in most cases a salary from your job. You apply that monthly income to your monthly expenses: rent or mortgage, car loan, food, gas, utilities, clothes, entertainment, etc. Our goal is to have our expenses be less than our income. Duh.

Over time, and with experience, we become better managers of our personal finances and begin to realize that we shouldn't spend more that we make. We strive to have some money left over at the end of the month that we can set aside and save. What we set aside and save is called **Retained Earnings**. Some of what we set aside we may **invest** with an eye toward future benefits. We may invest in stocks and bonds or mutual funds, or we may invest in education to expand our future earning and working prospects. This is the same type of money management discipline that is applied in business. It's just a matter of scale. There are a few additional zeros after the numbers on a large company's Income Statement but the idea is the same.

This concept applies to all businesses. Revenues are usually from Sales of products or services. Expenses are what you spend to support the operations: Salaries, raw materials, manufacturing processes and equipment, offices and factories, consultants (like a good accountant), lawyers, advertising, shipping, utilities etc. What is left over is the Net Income or Profit. Again: Revenues – Expenses = Net Income. Your Income needs to be more than your Outflow or your Upkeep is your Downfall. My Mom used to say that. :)

Net income is either saved in order to smooth out future operations and plan for unforeseen events; or invested in new plant, equipment, and technology; or paid out to the owners as a **dividend**.

On the next page is a sample Income Statement.

JJC Corporation

Income Statement

For the Year Ended

December 31, 2013

(In Millions of Dollars)

Revenues

Sales Revenues	2306
Service Revenues	1066
Total Revenues	3372

Expenses

Cost of Goods Sold Expense	1492
Selling, General, and Administrative Expense	983
Research & Development Expense	505
Interest Expense	54
Total Expenses	3034
Pre Tax Income	338
Income Tax Expense @ 22%	74
Net Income	264

The Income Statement is also known as the "profit and loss statement" or "statement of revenue and expense." Professionals sometimes use the shorthand term "P&L," which stands for profit and loss statement. A manager is said to have "P&L responsibilities" if they run an autonomous division. **P & L responsibility** is one of the most important responsibilities of any executive position and involves monitoring the net income after expenses for a department or entire organization, with direct influence on how company resources are allocated. The terms "profits," "earnings" and "net income" all mean the same thing and are used interchangeably.

Remember: Income (revenue or sales) – Expenses = Net Income or profit

Google the term "income statement" and you will see lots of examples of formats and presentations.

Financing Negative Income

There are situations where a company may have more expenses than revenue to cover them. In many cases this situation reflects a poorly operating company that is ultimately unsustainable.   But in some cases negative net income or cash flow can be part of sensible operations or strategy.   One such case that is common in operating a business occurs when revenues are lagging in accounts receivable and bills come due or salaries need to be paid.   Many expenses are regular and repeating like salaries, but revenues are often much more variable and unpredictable.   For this reason, most companies use a **line of credit** from their bank to smooth out these short term cash shortfalls.   This revolving credit instrument needs to be used judiciously.   It should only be used if there are accounts receivable in the offing that can repay it within the following thirty or sixty days max.

To make the analogy to our personal lives, credit cards are a personal form of a line of credit.   In learning to manage our money, it is common to have a few tough experiences with managing debt and its consequences. Personal debt usually occurs when we attempt to augment our income by using credit cards and spend more than we make.   Incurring debt is seductively easy. Monthly payments can quickly become a burden and the situation becomes increasingly difficult to favorably resolve.

Loans are described as debt with a fixed structure. It is structured with a set term such as five years with equal installment payments of interest and principal. At the end of the term both the **principal** (the amount you borrowed) and the interest have been paid off. Debt can be used to finance assets.

Debt is sometimes referred to as **leverage**. In analyzing a balance sheet leverage refers to the ratio of a company's loan capital (debt) to the value of its common stock (equity). Leverage can be a powerful business tool. But as we may learn navigating our personal finances it can also be seductive and dangerous. Especially if the assets purchased with debt lose their value. The financial crisis and recession starting in 2007 was a result of sophisticated and interconnected debt instruments defaulting in a cascade through the financial and banking system. Smart business people are not immune to making bad decisions and choices.

Another situation that requires financing negative income is the strategy of incurring losses in order to gain market share. This is a strategic decision, where financing lagging receivables with a line of credit is tactical. The losses incurred while chasing market share, while not sustainable in the long term, can accumulate over several years. This situation is funded with equity, the selling of shares of stock in the company.

Debt is a category we keep track of on the Balance Sheet as a **Liability**. Assets can be financed with debt and equity or a combination of the two. These three items: assets, debt and equity are what constitute a Balance Sheet.

Balance Sheet

The Balance Sheet can be summarized as: Assets = Liabilities + Equity. These three **balance sheet** segments give interested parties an idea as to what a company owns (**assets**) and owes (**liabilities**), and the amount invested and accumulated by the shareholders (**equity**).

The Balance Sheet is a snapshot of the financial position of a company at a particular point in time. It is compiled at the end of the year or quarter. It is a summary of the Assets, Liabilities and Equity. Think of how your home is financed as simple balance sheet. The asset is the value of the house (determined by an appraisal or sale); the liability is the mortgage balance and the equity is the difference between the two. If the house is worth more than you owe, then you have positive equity. The same concepts apply to a corporate balance sheet. If the assets are greater than the liabilities then there is positive shareholder's equity. If the liabilities are more than the assets, the company is considered insolvent. The same applies if your home mortgage is more than the value of the house. This situation is referred to as "upside-down" or "under water".

Balance Sheet Presentation

A Balance Sheet is constructed of two parts. Assets are listed in a column and totaled at the bottom of the column. Liabilities and Equity are listed in another column with the liabilities section listed above the equity section. Liabilities and Equity are each totaled separately and then together at the bottom. Sometimes these columns are presented in a stacked form with the Asset column on top. And sometimes these columns are presented side by side with the Assets on the left hand side and both Liabilities and Equity on the right hand side. When someone talks about the left hand side of the balance sheet, they are referring to Assets; if they talk about the right hand side of the balance sheet, they mean liabilities and equity. Liabilities and Equity totals in the right hand column must exactly equal the Asset total at the bottom of the left hand column. For comparison purposes, the Balance Sheet numbers of the previous year are also usually presented.. Remember the goal of these Financial Statements is to present the financial information in a clear and meaningful way so interested parties can quickly grasp the performance of the company.

According to GAAP, the U.S. accounting standard, assets and liabilities are listed in the order of their liquidity, from short term to long term, as you go down the items listed in each column. Cash is the most liquid asset so it is listed on the top left of the Balance Sheet. Long term debt comes after short term debts in the Liability Column and Equity is listed below the Liabilities. Equity is listed below Liabilities because shareholders have a junior claim on the assets of the corporation. In case of a bankruptcy or liquidation of the company, the money collected from the sale of assets goes first to pay the lenders. Any residual money after the lenders are paid off is distributed to the shareholders.

On the following page you find an example of a Balance Sheet. Since they vary in their contents and presentation it is a good idea to take a quick look at a bunch of examples. Google the term "balance sheet" and you will see lots of examples in various formats and presentations.

XYZ COMPANY
Balance Sheet
12/31/2017

ASSETS
Current Assets:

Cash	$12,000
Accounts Receivable	35,000
Inventory	120,000
Prepaid Rent	8,000
Total Current Assets	$175,000

Long-Term Assets

Land	$126,000
Buildings & Improvements	300,000
Furniture & Fixtures	50,000
General Equipment	125,000
Total Fixed Assets	$601,000

TOTAL ASSETS	**$776,000**

LIABILITIES
Current Liabilities:

Accounts Payable	$60,000
Taxes Payable	25,000
Salaries/Wages Payable	30,000
Interest Payable	25,000
Total Current Liabilities	$140,000

Long Term Liabilities:

Loan 1	$322,000
Total Long Term Liabilities	$322,000
TOTAL LIABILITIES	**$462,000**

OWNER'S EQUITY

Paid in Capital	$64,000
Retained Earnings	250,000
TOTAL OWNER'S EQUITY	**$314,000**

TOTAL LIABILITIES & OWNER'S EQUITY	**$776,000**

Assets and Depreciation

Assets are listed on the left hand side of the balance sheet. There are liquid assets such as cash, marketable securities, and Accounts Receivable. These are called **Current Assets**. Many assets are long lived items like equipment, vehicles, factories, and machines. These are called **Fixed Assets**. A significant amount of money is spent when fixed assets are purchased. Fixed assets have a shelf life that is significantly longer than the year in which they are purchased. For these reasons fixed assets are **capitalized** at their cost and each year of their proposed useful life a portion of the price is expensed to show how much of the asset was "used" in that year. This concept is called **Depreciation**. It provides a more accurate picture of how the operating assets of a company are contributing to the operations and spreads the expense through the years of its useful life when the asset is contributing to generating revenues. .

For example if we buy a machine that is assumed to last five years for $50,000 we would record this transaction and list the machine on the Balance Sheet at $50,000 as a Fixed Asset. Each year we would reduce that number by $10,000 of depreciation. So in the second year the asset would show up as being worth $40,000; $30,000 in the third year and so on. The number shown on the balance sheet is the original asset at cost, less (net of) depreciation. Assets are not listed individually on the Balance Sheet but are aggregated together and shown as a total number.

This is one reason why we need a Cash Flow Statement. The $50,000 would reduce our cash position in the first year and that would show up in the Investment section of the Cash Flow Statement. Each subsequent year, the $10,000 depreciation expense listed in the Income Statement would be added back in the Cash Flow Statement because it was not a cash expense in that year. It was just an accounting expense to keep track of the amount we are allocating to the "use" of the machine.

Amortization is similar to depreciation. Depreciation is used for tangible assets and amortization is used for intangible assets such as intellectual property like patents and trademarks. Amortization roughly matches an asset's expense with the revenue it generates. Amortization can also refer to the paying off of debt with a fixed repayment schedule in regular installments over a period of time.

These types of non-cash events are what are compensated for in the Cash Flow Statement in order to accurately reconcile the financial statements to how much cash is in the bank. We will discuss the Cash Flow Statement in more detail after we finish talking about the right side of the Balance Sheet: Liabilities and Equity.

Liabilities

Liabilities are claims against the company's assets. These claims are categorized as current or noncurrent. Current liabilities are ones that will come due within the year. Liabilities consist of obligations the enterprise owes to others. Along with Equity, they are how assets are funded. The debt can be to an unrelated third party, such as a bank, or to employees for wages earned but not yet paid. Accounts payable, payroll liabilities, and notes payable are examples of Liabilities.

Both assets and liabilities are categorized as current and noncurrent. This distinction is essential for the user of the financial statements to perform ratio analysis. We will discuss ratio and other financial statement analysis techniques later in this book.

Current Liabilities

Current liabilities are ones the company expects to settle within 12 months of the date on the balance sheet. Assets are used to pay these liabilities. The money can come from revenues generated from sales, or from current assets such as cash in the bank account.

The most common Current Liabilities are accounts payable. Any money a company owes its vendors for supplies or services, or to employees in the form of wage, or the government for taxes is considered a current liability. Most companies accrue payroll and related payroll taxes, which means the company owes them but has not yet paid them. All these types of obligations are acknowledged by the company and are intended to be settled in the relative near term.

Loans due in less than 12 months after the balance sheet date are also current liabilities. For example, a business may need a brief bridge loan in order to meet a payroll expense. Often this is structured as a line of credit with the expectation that the LOC will be paid off from the collection of accounts receivable or the sale of inventory.

Current portion of long-term notes payable is also considered a current liability. A long-term note will be paid back in full after that 12-month period. However, you must show the current portion, that which will be paid back in the current operating period, as a current liability.

Unearned revenue is a category that includes money the company has collected from customers but hasn't yet earned by performing the work. The company anticipates completing the tasks and earning the income within 12 months of the date of the balance sheet.

Long Term Liabilities

Noncurrent or long-term liabilities are ones the company doesn't expect to be liquidating or settling within 12 months of the balance sheet date. Businesses use debt to finance their activities and assets. These are structured as loans, notes, or bonds with interest and principal payments over the term. A business is financed by a mixture of debt and equity. This is called the capital structure of the company.

Stockholders' Equity

Stockholder's Equity, along with liabilities, can be thought of as the funding sources of the company's assets. The stockholders are the owners of the company. The ownership of a corporation is divided into **stock** or shares. There is an amount of shares authorized for the company when is created. This amount of authorized shares can be increased by a vote of the existing shareholders. A corporation raises money by selling shares. The amount of shares issued and sold is called the Shares Outstanding. This represents 100% of the ownership of the corporation. The amount of money raised and the amount of shares issued is tabulated and displayed in the Equity section of the Balance Sheet.

Stockholder's equity is equal to the asset amounts reported on the balance sheet minus the reported liability amounts. Equity is the residual of assets minus liabilities. In order to understand this think of the basic accounting equation:

$$Assets = Liabilities + Equity$$

And rearrange it to solve for Equity

$$Equity = Assets - Liabilities$$

In a corporation there may be more than one type of stock issued. These classes of stock will have different rights relative to voting and claims on assets and as such will have different values. In simple terms we can classify stock into two types: Common and Preferred.

Common Stock is the type of stock that forms the ownership of every corporation. Shares of common stock provide evidence of ownership in a corporation. Holders of common stock elect the corporation's directors and share in the distribution of profits of the company via dividends. If the corporation goes bankrupt and liquidates, the secured lenders are paid first, followed by unsecured lenders, preferred stockholders, and lastly the common stockholders.

Another financing instrument that corporations can issue in addition to their common stock is preferred stock. **Preferred Stock** is a class of stock that provides for preferential treatment of dividends. The preferred dividend can be thought of like interest on a loan. Preferred stockholders will be paid dividends before the common stockholders receive dividends. These dividends are sometimes paid in stock instead of money.

Both the common and preferred stock accounts are separated into two categories: Par Value and Additional Paid-in Capital or APIC. The bulk of the money is allocated to APIC. The Par Value account is a way to keep track of the amount of shares outstanding. The par value is a small monetary value attributed to each share. It is an arbitrary number, usually $.01. So if the company has 1,000 shares outstanding there would be $100.00 in the par value account. Par Value may also be $0.001. Par Value has no connection to the market value of the share of stock.

The Additional Paid-in Capital (APIC) account is where the amount paid for a share of stock, less the par value, is recorded. When a share of common stock having a par value of $0.01 is issued for $15, the account Common Stock will be credited for $0.01 and the corresponding Additional Paid-in Capital or APIC account will be credited for $14.99 (and Cash will be debited for $15.00).

Retained Earnings is the stockholders' equity account that records and reports the net income of a corporation from its inception until the balance sheet date less the dividends declared from its inception to the date of the balance sheet. This account tracks the profits or losses accumulated since a business was opened. The profits and losses accrue to the shareholders. At the end of each year, the profit or loss calculated on the income statement is used to adjust the value of this account. In an analogy from your personal life, think of Retained Earnings as your savings left over after you have paid all your expenses.

Contra Accounts

A contra account offsets the balance in another, related account with which it is paired. If the related account is an asset account, then a contra asset account is used to offset it with a credit balance. If the related account is a liability or equity account, then a contra liability or equity account is used to offset it with a debit balance. Stockholders' equity accounts normally have credit balances.

Contra equity accounts are a category of equity accounts with debit balances. A debit balance in an owner's equity account is contrary (contra) to an equity account's usual credit balance. An example of a contra stockholders' equity account is **Treasury Stock**. Treasury stock is a corporation's own stock that has been repurchased from stockholders and is being held by the corporation. Because it is stock that is outstanding but not in the hands of shareholders, it needs to be subtracted from the value of the outstanding stockholder's shares in order to properly value the equity. This is the purpose of a contra account. Depreciation is an asset contra account that reduces the value of an asset in a similar way.

We have now discussed the major accounts equity accounts. Some may be named differently but these synonyms represent the same functions. The stockholders' equity section of a corporation's balance sheet will look like this:

Stockholder's Equity

Paid-in capital

    Common Stock

    Preferred Stock

    Additional Paid-in Capital – Common Stock

    Additional Paid-in Capital – Preferred Stock

    Additional Paid-in Capital – Treasury Stock

Retained Earnings

Less: Treasury Stock

      Total Stockholder's Equity

Owner's Equity vs. Company's Market Value

Since the asset amounts reported on the Balance sheet are the cost of the assets at the time of the transaction, less depreciation, (their book value) they do not reflect current fair market values. The market value is how much you could sell the asset for or how much it would cost to replace. For example, a machine which cost $100,000 four years ago may now have a book value of $60,000. However, the current value of the machine might be just $15,000. An office building purchased by the company five years ago at a cost of $14,000,000 may now have a book value of $50,000,000. However, the current value of the building on the books with depreciation might be $10,000,000. Another example is Marketable Securities that were purchased for $2,000,000 but are now only worth a tenth of that. Since the assets are reported at their book value on the balance sheet and not reported at their current fair market value, the assets can be grossly under, or over, valued. This will affect the value of owner's equity since what appears on the balance sheet is not an indication of the fair market value of the company. In order to arrive at a realistic value of the equity, one must calculate market values of all the assets and subtract the liabilities from that total number. Remember Assets – Liabilities = Equity.

Fair value accounting takes a different approach to valuing assets and liabilities that can under the right circumstances provide a more accurate assessment of equity. **Mark-to-market** or fair value accounting refers to accounting for an asset or liability based on the current market price for similar assets or liabilities. The key here is that there must be an active, liquid, and measurable market upon which to make the assessment. Fair value accounting has been a part of Generally Accepted Accounting Principles (GAAP) in the United States since the early 1990s.

Mark-to-market accounting changes values on the balance sheet as market conditions change. In contrast, historical cost accounting, based on the past transactions, is simpler, more stable, and easier to perform, but does not represent current market value. Instead, it summarizes past transactions and historical prices.

Mark to market accounting needs market transaction information in order to work. When markets dry up or freeze such as in 2008 it is difficult to value assets based on this approach. Mark-to-market accounting can become volatile if market prices fluctuate greatly or change unpredictably.

Temporary Accounts

Revenues, expenses, and the resulting gain or loss are income statement accounts. The income statement accounts are called temporary accounts because they reset to zero each year after they are reconciled to Retained Earnings. The gain or loss from the income statement is resolved to the Retained Earnings in the Equity section of the Balance Sheet. Revenues and gains cause owner's equity to increase. Expenses and losses cause owner's equity to decrease.

Cash Flow Statement (the other financial statement)

Besides the Income Statement and the Balance Sheet, there is a third financial statement called the **Cash Flow Statement**. The Cash Flow Statement reconciles the Income Statement with the actual cash position of the company (the balance in the bank account) by adding and subtracting revenues and expenses that were properly recorded on the Income Statement, but are non-cash events. Depreciation and Accounts Receivable are examples of non-cash events. This reconciled bank account balance is the number that then is used for the Cash account at the top of the asset column on the Balance Sheet. This is important. This is how the financial statements are interconnected.

The need for a Cash Flow Statement arises from Accrual Accounting where we book Receivables and Payables and Depreciation in order to provide a more accurate picture of the operations of a company by matching revenues and expenses. These "non-cash" transactions distort the Income Statement relative to how much cash actually came in and went out of the company and how much is actually in the bank. The Operations portion of the Cash Flow Statement reconciles these differences.

Besides Operations, there are two other parts of the Cash Flow Statement that follow the Operations portion: Investing and Financing. The Investing section shows the money that was spent on capital equipment items that don't show up as expenses on the Income Statement because they have been capitalized as Assets. The Financing section primarily shows money that has come into the company through the sale of stock or through a loan.

The concepts behind the Cash Flow Statement are a nuanced and might be confusing to someone familiarizing themselves with the basic principles of accounting for the first time. It might be wise learn more about the Cash Flow Statement after one has a solid handle on the basics. For now, just be aware that there is such a thing as a Cash Flow Statement and what its basic functions and purpose are.

Interconnections and Flow

The three Financial Statements are interconnected. Basically you start a year with a Balance Sheet showing the financial position at the beginning of the period; next you have the Income Statement that shows the operations during the year period, and then a balance Sheet at the end of the year. The Cash Flow reconciles the cash position from the Income Statement and that cash number is used as the Cash account balance at the top right of the end of year (EOY) Balance Sheet.

Think of it as a system of two Balance Sheets acting as book-ends for the Income Statement. And the Cash Flow Statement used to reconcile the Net Income (or Loss) at the bottom of the Income Statement with the amount of cash actually in the bank. This cash number is used in the Cash account on the second end of year Balance Sheet.

This section, though short, ties together the functionality of the financial statements. This might be an "aha" moment for you. It was for me when I finally realized how this all fit and worked together.

Financial Statement Analysis

Accounting and Finance overlap in this area. The launching place for Corporate Finance is the ability to read and understand Financial Statements. The analysis of financial statements and subsequent assumptions and projections based on that analysis is the next step. **Financial statement analysis** is the process of analyzing a company's financial statements and comparing the analysis across companies and industries in order to make better operating and investing decisions. This analysis method involves specific techniques for evaluating and quantifying risk, performance, financial health, and the future prospects of an enterprise. We can look at the performance of a particular company over time such as year to year results. This is called **Horizontal Analysis**. And we can look at various performance characteristics within a single time period.

This is called **Vertical Analysis**. We can create metrics across an industry segment as an average value to compare our company against. This is called **Benchmarking**. We can also aggregate up different industry groups and see how they perform relative to each other. This type of analysis can be helpful in gauging where to allocate investment dollars in a portfolio. It can also be used to see how a management team is performing relative to its competition.

Financial Statements are analyzed and scrutinized by a variety of stakeholders including debt and equity investors, government agencies and taxing authorities, and management decision-makers. It is what credit analysts do. These stakeholders have different interests and apply a variety of different techniques to meet their needs. For example, some equity investors are more interested in the long-term earnings power of the organization and perhaps the sustainability and growth of dividend payments. Some equity investors like hedge funds may be looking for latent risks and pitfalls in order to capitalize on a short position. This means they are looking for companies about to collapse. Creditors want to ensure that interest and principal on the organization's debt securities are paid on time and when due. Banks and commercial lenders use financial statement analysis as part of their credit analysis to determine whether or not to make loans and lend. Ratings Agencies such as Moody's, Standard and Poors, and Fitch perform financial statement analysis in order to rate the risk and creditworthiness of companies and their debt. Managers use it to see how their company is performing relative to historical performance, their targets, and their industry.

Techniques of financial statement analysis include **fundamental analysis**, the use of **financial ratios** and DuPont analysis. Analysis methods are performed in a horizontal or vertical fashion across a company.

In order to project future performance, historical information is used combined with assumptions about the prospect for the company and the future economic environment. This stream of profits from future years is what is used to calculate the value of a business. This is the foundational concept of **Business Valuation** and **Corporate Finance**.

Before we get into the nitty-gritty of these techniques, let's start with an historical overview of how financial statement analysis developed and has evolved.

History of Financial Statement Analysis

The stock market crash in October 1929 was a catastrophic event that led to the Great Depression and worldwide economic strife. It also led to social unrest and political turmoil. These events called into question the viability of Capitalism and Democracy as unsettling systemic flaws were exposed and many, many people suffered.

A major basis of the problem was that many companies who traded on the stock market did not provide meaningful information about the state of their business. There were no financial statements to review. There was no transparency. In order to clean up the mess and maintain investor confidence in the stock market, the

Roosevelt administration created the **Securities and Exchange Commission** (SEC) to regulate and oversee the stock market. Roosevelt needed someone to run the SEC who knew all the dirty tricks of the stock market so they could effectively identify and combat abuse.. The man who rose to the occasion was Joseph P. Kennedy, John F. Kennedy's father; a famous stock manipulator and patriot.

Part of the SEC's new rules were that every traded company had to have financial statements prepared by an outside third party auditing firm under a rigorous set of accounting rules called **GAAP,** Generally Accepted Accounting Principles. These financial statements along with disclosures about the operations had to be filed and made publicly available through the SEC each and every year. That document is called a **10K**. This kind of disclosure and transparency, allows investors and the public to understand a company's operations and prospects and make determinations about whether or not to invest.

This set of regulations seems obvious and eminently sensible now, but it was bold, and brilliant, and a revelation at the time. **Fundamental analysis,** a system of analyzing this new information, came to prominence almost immediately. To this day, the **10K** is the basic document and fundamental analysis is the tool set for stock market analysis and corporate investment decision making.

Fundamental Analysis

The SEC and financial reporting regulations were instituted in two legislations: the '33 Act and the '34 Act. Benjamin Graham and David Dodd first published their influential book "Security Analysis" in 1934. Warren Buffett is a well-known disciple of Graham and Dodd's philosophy.

The Graham and Dodd approach is referred to as Fundamental Analysis and includes: Economic analysis; Industry analysis; and Company analysis. Company Analysis is the primary realm of financial statement analysis. On the basis of these three analyses the value of the security is determined. Fundamental analysis is how bankers, analysts, and investors make long-term investment decisions.

Their book has gone through many revisions and editions and is available in a recently revised edition. You may want to check it out; especially if you have any aspirations to be like Warren. Another proponent of Graham and Dodd is Bill Ackman the American hedge fund manager. He is the founder and CEO of **Pershing Square Capital Management**. Bill is also a billionaire.

Here is the information on the book:

Dodd, David; Graham, Benjamin (1998). **Security Analysis**. John Wiley & Sons, Inc. ISBN 0-07-013235-6.

Horizontal and Vertical Analysis

Horizontal analysis compares financial information over time, typically from past financial statements such as the income statement. When comparing this past information we look for variations of particular line items such as higher or lower earnings, sales revenues, or particular expenses. Horizontal analysis is used to look for trends that can be extrapolated in order to predict future performance.

Vertical analysis is a proportional analysis performed on financial statements. It is ratio analysis. Line items of interest on the financial statement are listed as a percentage of another line item. For example, on an income statement each line item will be listed as a percentage of Sales.

Financial Ratios

Financial ratios are powerful tools used to assess company upside, downside, and risk. There are four main categories of ratios: liquidity ratios, profitability ratios, activity ratios and leverage ratios. These are typically analyzed over time and across competitors in an industry. Using ratios "normalizes" the numbers so you can compare companies in apples-to-apples terms.

Liquidity and Solvency

Solvency and liquidity are both refer to a company's financial health and viability. Solvency refers to an enterprise's capacity to meet its long-term financial commitments. Liquidity refers to an enterprise's ability to par short-term obligations. Liquidity is also a measure of how quickly assets can be sold to raise cash.

A solvent company is one that owns more than it owes. It has a positive net worth and is carrying a manageable debt load. A company with adequate liquidity may have enough cash available to pay its bills, but may still be heading for financial disaster down the road. In this case a company meets liquidity standards by is not solvent. Healthy companies are both solvent and possess adequate liquidity.

Liquidity ratios are used to determine whether a company has enough current asset capacity to pay its bills and meet its obligations in the foreseeable future (current liabilities). **Solvency ratios** are a measure of how quickly a company can turn its assets into cash if it experiences financial difficulties or is threatened with bankruptcy. Both measure different aspects of if, and how long, a company can pay its bills and remain in business.

The current ratio and the quick ratio are two common liquidity ratios. The **current ratio** is current assets/current liabilities and measures how much liquidity (cash) is available to address current liabilities (bills and other obligations). The **quick ratio** is (current assets – inventories) / current liabilities. The quick ratio measures a company's ability to meet its short-term obligations based on its most liquid assets, and therefore excludes inventories from its current assets. It is also known as the "acid-test ratio."

The **solvency ratio** is used to examine the ability of a business to meet its long-term obligations. The ratio is most commonly used by lenders and bankers. The ratio compares cash flows to liabilities. The solvency ratio calculation involves the following steps:

All non-cash expenses are added back to after-tax net income. This approximates the amount of cash flow generated by the business. You can find the numbers to add back in the Operations section of the Cash Flow Statement.

Add together all short-term and long-term obligations. This is the Total Liabilities number on the Balance Sheet. Then divide the estimated cash flow figure by the liabilities total.

The formula for the ratio is:

(Net after-tax income + Non-cash expenses)/(Short-term liabilities + Long-term liabilities)

A higher percentage indicates an increased ability to support the liabilities of a business over the long-term.

Remember that estimations made over a long term are inherently inaccurate. There are many variables that can impact the ability to pay over the long term. Using any ratio to estimate solvency needs to be taken with a grain of salt.

Profitability ratios are ratios help discern how profitable a company is. To be profitable, a company has to cover costs. The breakeven point and the gross profit ratio address the dynamics of cost coverage in different ways. The breakeven point calculates how much cash a company must generate to break even with their operating costs. The gross profit ratio is equal to (revenue - the cost of goods sold)/revenue. This ratio provides a quick snapshot of expected revenue that can be applied to the overhead expenses and fixed costs of operations.

Some additional examples of profitability ratios are profit margin, return on assets and return on equity. The higher the value in these ratios, the more profitable a company is. Having a higher value relative to a competitor's ratio or the same ratio from a previous period is indicative that the company is performing relatively well and going in the right direction.

Activity ratios are calculated to show how well management is doing managing the company's resources. Activity ratios measure company sales relative to another asset account. The most common asset accounts used are accounts receivable, inventory, and total assets. Since most companies have a lot of resources tied up in accounts receivable, inventory and working capital, these accounts are used in the denominator of the most common activity ratios.

Accounts receivable (AR) is the total amount of money due to a company for products or services sold on a credit account. The length of time until AR is collected is critical because that expected revenue must be financed in some way. The accounts receivable turnover shows how rapidly a company collects what is owed to it and indicates the liquidity of the receivables.

Accounts Receivable Turnover = Total Credit Sales/Accounts Receivable

The average collection period in days, equal to 365 days divided by the accounts receivable turnover is another ratio that helps gain insight into AR collection:

Average Collection Period = 365 Days/Accounts Receivable Turnover

Analysts frequently use the average collection period to measure the effectiveness of a company's ability to collect payments from its credit customers. The average collection period should be less than the credit terms that the company extends to its customers.

A significant indicator of profitability is the ability to manage inventory. Inventory is money and resources invested that do not earn a return until the product is sold. The longer inventory sits, the less profitable a company can be. A higher inventory turnover ratio indicates more demand for products, better cash management and also the reduced risk of inventory obsolescence. The best measure of inventory utilization is the inventory turnover ratio. It is calculated as either the total annual sales, or the cost of goods sold (COGS), divided by the cost of inventory.

Inventory Turnover = Total Annual Sales or Cost of Goods Sold/Inventory Cost

Using the cost of goods sold in the numerator can provide a more accurate indicator of inventory turnover because it allows a more direct comparison with other companies. Different companies have different markups to the sale price and this can obscure apples-to-apples comparison.

The average inventory cost is usually used in the denominator to compensate for seasonal differences.

Leverage ratios analyze the degree to which a company uses debt to finance its operations and assets. The debt-to-equity ratio is the most common. This ratio is calculated as:

(Long-term debt + Short-term debt + Leases)/ Equity

Companies with high debt ratios need to have steady and predictable revenue streams in order to service that debt. Companies whose revenues fluctuate and are less predictable should rely more on equity in its capital structure. Leverage also has obvious implications for solvency.

DuPont analysis was developed by the **DuPont Corporation** in the 1920s as a tool to assess their investments across their various companies and operations. As an early conglomerate, they need a tool to assess the relative performance of varied business in order to make decisions of where and how to allocate resources. By now it has been widely adopted as a managerial and investment tool.

DuPont Analysis is an expression which breaks return on equity (ROE) into three parts.

The basic formula is:

ROE = (Profit margin)*(Asset turnover)*(Equity multiplier) =

(Net profit/Sales)*(Sales/Assets)*(Assets/Equity)
= (Net Profit/Equity)

The three constituent parts are:

- Profitability: measured by profit margin
- Operating efficiency: measured by asset turnover
- Financial leverage: measured by equity multiplier

DuPont analysis enables you to understand the source of superior (or inferior) return by comparison with companies in similar industries or between industries. It also provides a deeper level of understanding by parsing apart the significant variable of return on equity. And ROE is certainly a metric that equity investors find important.

Working Capital

Working Capital is a term used to describe the amount of money and liquid assets available and required to operate a business. It is a financial metric which represents operating liquidity. Working capital is the difference between current assets and current liabilities.

Along with fixed assets such as plant and equipment, working capital is considered a part of operating capital. The management of working capital involves managing inventories, accounts receivable, accounts payable, and cash.

Current assets and current liabilities include three accounts which are of special importance. These accounts represent the areas of the business where managers have the most direct impact and influence:

- Accounts receivable (current asset)
- Inventory (current assets), and
- Accounts payable (current liability)

Short-term loans and the current portion of long-term debt (payable within 12 months) are also critical, because they represent short-term claims on current assets and are often secured by long-term assets. Bank loans and lines of credit are common types of short-term debt

An increase in net working capital indicates that the business has either increased current assets or has decreased current liabilities. Financing and managing working capital is a major operating challenge, especially for companies that are rapidly growing.

Financing Working Capital

Receivables and inventory are usually financed with a line of credit (revolving debt like a credit card). Managing receivables aims at making sure that all your customers pay and that they pay in a timely manner; you need that cash in the door! Accounts Receivables turnover is a ration we discussed earlier that indicates the timeliness of credit sales being paid.

Managing inventories a means not letting inventories build up. You do this by monitoring sales, manufacturing activity, and the Inventory turnover ratio. You want enough inventories so you can accommodate a spike in sales, but you also don't want to risk having too much inventory that you can't unload. This is especially important with products that have a short life cycle and can become obsolete. If not sold in a timely manner this might force you to deeply discount products in order to sell them. This can lead to incurring a loss. Operations Management is the discipline focused on these issues and mitigating potential problems.

You can quickly asses how a company is doing in this regard by looking at their balance sheet and comparing Current Assets to Current Liabilities and seeing if there is a larger amount of Current Assets. Do this comparison for the last few years and you can see if there is a change in Working Capital and if it is due to a build-up of inventories.

Finding Financial Statements to Read and Understand

Now you know what information is conveyed in Financial Statements are, how they are structured and presented, and techniques for analyzing them. You can now use this knowledge to look up, review and analyze companies. Look at other businesses in your line of work and compare how your company is doing in comparison to them. Or check out companies you might be interested in investing in. You can find tons of such information online related to publicly traded companies.

Company Specific Financial Information

Public companies are corporations that are traded on the stock market. Most large companies you are familiar with are publicly traded. Their stock price is listed in the paper and on Yahoo! Finance and other websites. The Securities and Exchange Commission (SEC) regulates these companies and the stock markets. One of the requirements for these companies is to submit audited financial statements along with descriptive information about their operations to the SEC. These annual reports, called 10Ks, are available online for public review. You can now begin to put your new found knowledge to use.

Look on the www.SEC.gov website for 10Ks of public companies. Besides their annual financial statements, public companies must also disclose information about their operations and strategy such as:

- Who they believe their competitors are,
- How they plan to grow the business,

- What the general economy looks like and

- How they predict it will affect their business segments.

This represents a wealth of expert opinion on your specific business domain and makes for great and profitable reading

The Role of Auditors

As per the SEC requirements and regulations, in order to be eligible to be traded on a stock exchange, a publicly traded company's financials must be prepared by the company and then reviewed and audited by an outside Certified Public Accountant (CPA).

What is an auditor?

The auditing process entails reviewing the financial statements prepared and drafted by the company to make sure they conform to GAAP and other rules. The auditors also "test" the numbers by requesting and reviewing supporting documentation such as invoices, checks, bills, and contracts. They send letters to the company's banks to confirm bank balances and contact lawyers the company has worked with to confirm that there are no liabilities or law suits pending that have not been disclosed.

The Auditing Process

As we have discussed, there are strong temptations to commit fraud. People who run companies have the power to exploit financial information for personal gain. For publicly traded companies annual auditing is a legal requirement. The investors of many privately held companies, including their bankers, also require annual audited financial statements.

The audit process is designed to protect against misrepresenting financial information to improve results, avoid taxation, hide fraud, or not report latent liabilities. Audits are a process of gaining information about the financial systems and the financial records of a company.

Financial audits are performed to ascertain the validity and reliability of information, as well as to provide an assessment of the company's internal control system. Audits are carried out by a third party impartial account that is certified as a CPA.

To work on other company's financials you must be a CPA. In the United States a CPA will have passed the Uniform Certified Public Accountant Examination and met additional state education and experience requirements for membership in thier state's professional accounting body. You don't have to be a CPA to work for a company internally as an employee in accounting or finance.

Since the auditor cannot feasibly know or discover everything about a company, an audit seeks to provide reasonable assurance that the financial statements are free from material error. Test work and sampling of documents is performed in audits as a way to statistically confirm that the accounting has been done properly by the company. A set of financial statements are understood to be 'true and fair' when they are deemed free of material misstatements. The auditor confirms this in their opinion letter that precedes the financials in the presentation. The opinion given on financial statements depends on the audit evidence obtained. You find the opinion letter at the beginning of the audited financial statements.

GAAP and IFSR

GAAP is short for Generally Accepted Accounting Principles. These are the rules and accounting principles that have been adopted by the accounting profession in the United States. The rest of the world has adopted a different set of standards called IFSR. IFSR stands for International Financial Reporting Standards. It is the accounting standard used in more than 110 countries. Both standards intend to capture and represent the economics of accounting transactions as accurately and clearly as possible.

The fact that there are two different accounting frameworks in the world creates problems for users of accounting information and are a burden to international companies. International companies must keep two sets of accounting records and provide two completely different sets of audited financial statements. That ends up being a cumbersome amount of extra work. Although there has been an effort to harmonize the two standards into one universal standard, they have not arrived at one yet.

Budgeting

Budgets are financial projections developed for a relatively short and predetermined period of time. Most budgets are prepared for the next year and divided into detailed monthly budgets. Budgets can be expected to be reasonably accurate because they represent estimates of relatively short time periods and because they rely on historical information about the company.

Budgets are created, reviewed, and approved and then used to measure the actual performance of the company each month. Did the company under or over perform relative to the budget? The differences between the actual accounting prepared at the end of the month and the budget amounts is called a Variance. Variances are reviewed and discussed to see why some line items went over budget and why some may be significantly under budget. Budgets are developed using historical performance data, which means that they are relatively predictive of the levels at which a company should be operating. And the budget will reflect the goals that management hopes to achieve in the coming year.

Budgeting is part of the planning process and reviewing the actual results against the budget on a regular basis is good management practice.

Financial Projections

Financial projections are less accurate than budgets because they are forecasting sales and expenses three to five years into the future. The ability to predict the future with any level of accuracy diminishes as the timeframe gets more remote and removed from the present.

Financial projections are made for start-ups or new divisions of companies. This is done for long term planning and valuation purposes. Financial projections are used to assess whether a project is financially worth pursuing. They serve as an instrument to analyze whether or not to make an investment or fund a project or venture.

Spreadsheets

Budgets and Financial Projections are prepared in spreadsheets. The rows and columns are perfectly suited for a quick summation of revenues and expenses in columns and rows. The actual accounting figures can be imported into a spreadsheet from the accounting software for variance analysis.

Many of you are probably very familiar with spreadsheets and how they operate. Here is a short summary for those of you becoming familiar with them.

Spreadsheets are computer programs used a lot in accounting as worksheets. Arranged in the manner of a mathematical matrix, they contain a multicolumn, multi-row layout. Using them makes your life simple when adding columns of numbers and it gives you clear a record of those columns and calculations. This can be convenient six months later when you can't remember how the heck you came up with a certain number that is throwing your books out of whack.

Microsoft Excel is the most common spreadsheet program, both powerful and easy to learn. Become familiar with the basic functions and features of Excel. There are great online tutorials from Microsoft from absolute beginner through sophisticated applications of Excel. There are also many third party tutorials freely available on YouTube.

Managerial and Cost Accounting

What we have been discussing so far is called Financial Accounting: recording transactions and preparing financial statements. Another part of accounting is Cost Accounting. While Financial Accounting information is of interest to users both internal and external to the company, cost accounting is a set of techniques that is strictly applied and used only internally

The goal of cost accounting is to clearly understand the costs associated with the products produced and services provided by a company. Understanding costs in detail is extremely important in order to figure out the best and least expensive ways to make products.

Cost accounting is an important management decision making tool. Managers use cost accounting to make decisions to maximize profitability.

Differences between Financial and Cost Accounting

Financial accounting aims at recording and presenting the results of an accounting year in the form of an Income Statement, Balance Sheet, and Cash Flow Statement. Cost Accounting aims at computing the costs of production or services in a rigorous analytic manner that facilitates cost control and cost reduction.

Financial accounting reports the results and position of business to management, government, creditors, investors, and other external parties, while Cost Accounting is an internal reporting system to aid management in their decision making processes.

In financial accounting, cost classification is based on various types of transactions, such as salaries, repairs, insurance, inventory etc. In cost accounting, classification is made on the basis of functions, activities, products, and processes. It is a different approach and way of looking at costs and how they aggregate up. Cost accounting classifications and presentation is directed at internal planning and control and serves the information needs of the organization.

Financial accounting aims at presenting a 'true and fair' view of the transactions, profit and loss for a period, and the Balance Sheet on a given date.. These concepts are not the focus in cost accounting since we are not making reports to share with the general public.

What is Cost Accounting?

Managers need actionable information to make informed decisions about how to increase profits.

There are two ways to increase net income or profit:

- Increase revenues

- Reduce costs

Rarely can you increase revenues without also increasing costs to support the increased revenues. If costs increase at a faster rate than revenues increase, due to inefficiencies, then increasing revenues is counterproductive. Or in the second case, if a reduction in costs, say marketing of advertising, has an unintended negative impact on revenues, then that cost reduction strategy is also counterproductive. These scenarios illustrate the fundamental importance of really having a good handle on all the aspects of costs and the dynamics of how they vary.

Understanding cost structure and determining costs of producing goods or delivering services can get complicated. Complexity increases as the number of variables and components of cost increase. Complexity can vary depending on the scale of an operation, the degree of automation and labor, the number of inputs, and the complexity of overhead calculations and estimates. Cost accounting is a sub discipline of accounting that deals with measuring costs accurately. Cost Accounting is a function internal to the enterprise and not shared with the outside world like Financial Accounting.

Cost accounting is a process of collecting, analyzing, summarizing, and evaluating the various elements that make up the total costs of production and delivery. Cost accounting techniques are used to understand the cost structure and how different cost components vary with the amounts produced. Operations and production processes can be optimized with a greater understanding of cost structure.

Cost accounting is used to analyze different alternatives in order to make optimal decisions about the most cost efficient use of resources and production and distribution processes. Cost accounting has close ties to operation's management and industrial process design. You may be able to reduce costs by substituting less expensive materials, or streamlining a workflow in a manufacturing floor design.

Looking at it from an Income Statement point of view the goal of managing and controlling costs allows the maximum amount of revenue to fall to the bottom line as net income.

Cost accounting provides detailed cost information for management to control current operations and plan for the future. Its primary function is to facilitate decision making for managers. This is why cost accounting is sometimes called managerial accounting.

The goal is to produce reports or computer dashboards that are used by management to determine the most appropriate course of action based on the cost efficiency and production capability.

There is wide variety of approaches to cost accounting and the systems used by different companies and even in different parts of the same company or organization. Unlike the financial accounting systems that record the debits and credits of transactions and assist in the preparation of **periodic financial reports**, cost accounting systems and reports are not subject to rules and standards such as **Generally Accepted Accounting Principles**.

Financial Statements are shared with parties outside a company like bankers, investors, governmental authorities, and suppliers. Because they are shared with outsiders for them to make decisions about the health and profitability of a company, they need to be uniform, consistent, and adhere to certain standards.

Managerial and cost accounting reports are proprietary. They are not shared outside the company. There is more latitude and flexibility in preparing what information is important and how best to present it to be actionable.

How Costs are categorized

There are two basic types of accounting: managerial, also called cost, accounting, and financial accounting. Financial accounting is shared with the outside world in the form of reporting financial statements. Cost accounting is proprietary and only shared within a company. If done well, cost accounting is a competitive advantage.

In financial accounting we show costs as expenses on the Income Statement. Direct costs are sometimes shown as an expense line right below revenues. We call this expense line Cost of Goods Sold or COGS.

In cost accounting our focus is on what is costs to produce something. Our goal is to manage costs and optimize them. The less something costs to make, the more profit.

We bundle expenses to parse cost information so we can gain managerial insights. Our goal is to better analyze product or manufacturing costs.

We separate our costs into two general categories: direct and indirect costs. There are three basic elements of costs: direct materials, direct labor, and overhead. Materials and labor are the major components that make up direct costs. Overhead is an indirect cost. We group these all together as manufacturing costs.

In financial accounting we show costs as expenses on the Income Statement. Direct costs are sometimes shown as an expense line right below revenues. We call this expense line Cost of Goods Sold or COGS.

What gets measured gets managed, so measure what matters.

In cost accounting our focus is on what is costs to produce something. Our goal is to manage costs and optimize them. The less something costs to make, the more profit.

We bundle expenses to parse cost information so we can gain managerial insights. Our goal is to better analyze product or manufacturing costs.

We separate our costs into two general categories: direct and indirect costs. There are three basic elements of costs: direct materials, direct labor, and overhead. Materials and labor are the major components that make up direct costs. Overhead is an indirect cost. We group these all together as manufacturing costs.

Creating value is the process of transforming inputs into a product or service. The cost of raw materials and labor are what make up direct costs.

Direct materials include purchased parts. They are directly associated with making the product. There are materials that support the process but don't end up in the finished good. Things like oil for machines or masking tape for painting. These are indirect materials. We account for indirect materials as part manufacturing overhead.

Direct labor is the cost of the workers who make the product. Indirect labor includes workers who do not use the direct materials to build the product. Supervisors, managers, and maintenance workers are indirect labor. Indirect labor is part of manufacturing overhead.

Manufacturing overhead costs include indirect materials, indirect labor, and all other manufacturing costs. Depreciation on factory equipment is part of overhead. Costs related to the factory like rent, insurance, taxes, and utilities are also part of manufacturing overhead.

Direct, Indirect, Fixed and Variable Costs

This nomenclature is interrelated and can be confusing. You may have to read through this section a couple of times to refresh and clarify these concepts. It may be a bit confusing at first, but will become clear with use.

All types of businesses track their activities with cost accounting techniques. Managers need to understand the costs of running the business. If you don't know your costs accurately, you don't know if you are making money. You need to sell things for more than they cost to make to have a sustainable business.

Cost accounting developed with the **industrial revolution**. As the scale of enterprises increased so did their complexity. Operating complex enterprises led to the development of systems for recording and tracking costs. Understanding costs help managers make better decisions. We now have 300 years of cost accounting experience to draw upon.

In the beginning of the industrial age costs were primarily **variable costs**. Labor, raw materials, and power varied directly with the level of production. The total variable costs were a rough guide for decision-making.

Variable costs go up and down according to the volume of work. Other costs tend to remain the same whether a factory is busy or idle. Manufacturing has become more mechanized and automated. As a result, **fixed costs** have become more important in management.

Fixed costs include factories, equipment, and maintenance. They also include overhead costs like quality control, storage, plant supervision and engineering. These costs were not part of businesses in the early days of industrialization. With the growth of industrial scale enterprises like railroads, fixed costs became important. You can't move freight on a railroad without first putting down tracks and buying locomotives. These are fixed costs.

Not understanding how to allocate fixed costs to products initially lead to poor decision making. Today we know that understanding fixed costs is crucial to making informed decisions about products and pricing.

Direct costs such as labor and raw materials are variable costs. Total variable costs increase as more units are manufactured. For example, every pizza made in a pizzeria uses a certain amount of dough. That dough, the raw material, is a variable cost.

Direct costs can be variable or fixed. A supervisor is a *direct* cost. Her salary is the same each week no matter how many products are manufactured. Her salary is a *fixed* cost. By contrast, raw materials are a *direct* cost, and a **variable cost.** The amount of supplies used increases as the volume or activity increases. Got it?

Fuel used operating a machine is an indirect cost. The cost of the fuel is variable because more is used when the machine runs longer and more products are made. Depreciation is also an indirect cost. It is a fixed cost since the machine's depreciation expense is the same each year and not tied to its amount of use.

Costs are categorized as direct or indirect. The cost is fixed if the total amount of the cost does not change as production volume changes. If the cost changes as a function of activity or volume, it is a variable cost.

Classifying costs in these ways help managers understand the dynamics of their operations. It helps them use data about the past, in the present, to make better decisions about the future. A deep understanding of costs and their dynamics is a competitive advantage.

Classification of Costs

"The Secret of all victory lies in the organization of the nonobvious."

Marcus Aurelius

In cost accounting we classify and group costs according to their common characteristics. The basic characteristics are what we have just discussed.

There are four basic categories for organizing costs: element, traceability, function and structural. There are three elements of costing: material, labor and overhead. Traceability refers to Direct **and Indirect Costs**. Functions have to do with departments and how the operation is organized like production, administration, selling and distribution, and R&D. Structural classification means whether a cost is fixed or variable.

Allocating Indirect Costs

In order to allocate an indirect cost to a specific product, we need to determine a function or cost driver that will attribute the proper portion of the indirect cost to the product (cost object). This driver can be related to one of the direct inputs like labor or material, or calculated as a function of time. In this manner standard cost accounting typically determines indirect and overhead costs as a percentage of a direct cost. This is called activity-based costing.

There are two main approaches to aggregating up these costs depending on the manufacturing or production environment based on product or period. The product approach focuses on the product and the resources used to make and individual product. These costs then get accumulated based on how many products were manufactured. The period approach focuses on a period of time such as each month and is used for manufacturing processes that are continual such as producing breakfast cereal. It would not be efficient to analyze the inputs into each Cheerio. In these cases it is more efficient to look at the process flow and the volume produced during a specific time period and to use that as the cost driver for allocating indirect costs.

Inventory, WIP and COGS

The Product Cost approach takes raw materials and labor, both direct and indirect, and overhead, and adds them up in an account called **Work in Progress** or **WIP**. When materials are first purchased they are recorded in inventory accounts. As a product is created, more costs are added to the WIP account. When a product is completed, the WIP account transfers to a **finished goods inventory**. When an item is sold the finished goods inventory account transfers the costs to the Cost of Goods Sold account (COGS). COGS reflects all the direct, indirect, and overhead costs that have gone into making that product or delivering that service.

This procedure of developing a product with a WIP account outlines the flow through the journal accounts of the process of manufacturing.

Translating Cost Accounting to the Income Statement

COGS shows up on the Income Statement as the first line under Sales Revenue. It is subtracted from Sales Revenue in order to calculate Net Sales Revenue.

What COGS does not include are the administrative, sales, and marketing expenses that support the distribution and sales of products and also support the operation of the firm. These expenses are listed on the Income Statement after Net Sales Revenue and are totaled and subtracted from Net Sales in order to calculate Net Income.

Managerial Economics and Cost Accounting

The structure and dynamics of costs and revenues vary from one company to the next. They vary based on the volume produced and sold. Managerial economics and cost accounting overlap in measuring and analyzing these relationships.

The goal of managers is to maximize profit. Managerial economics is a set of tools to minimize costs and maximize revenues. It applies the techniques of microeconomics to total, average, and marginal costs. It determines levels of costs and revenues that optimize profit. Cost accounting and economics overlap in the field of managerial economics. We will now look at several very useful cost and revenue analysis techniques.

Break Even Analysis

The **break-even point** is a concept used in economics and business. It is derived from cost accounting data. It is the number where total costs, fixed and variable, and total revenue are equal. It is the number of units that need to be sold so there is no net loss or gain.

At break-even, all the costs are covered. The profit at the breakeven point is 0. This is the point after which additional sales will contribute to a profit.

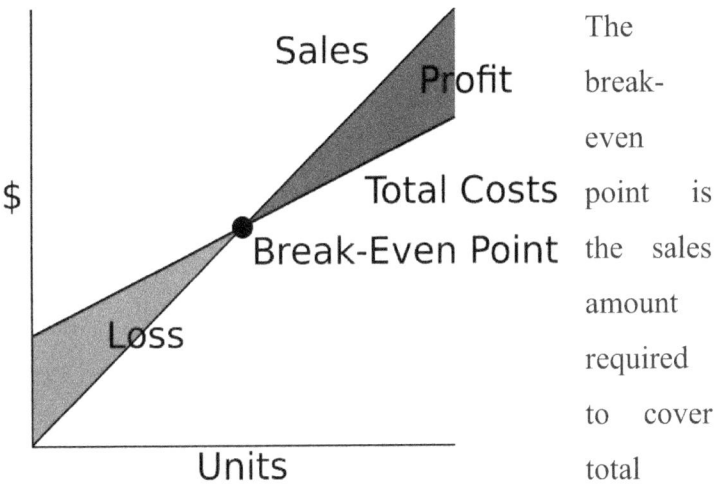

The break-even point is the sales amount required to cover total costs. Total costs are both fixed and variable costs. It can be measured either in units or revenue. Break-even is only possible if the price charged per unit is higher the variable cost per unit. The difference between price and variable cost contributes toward covering fixed costs. We call this amount the **Contribution Margin.**

The goal of business is to make a profit. **Break-even analysis** determines the sales that must be exceeded to make a profit. It is a measure of the sustainability of a business. It also measures the impact of marketing campaigns.

The break-even point is clear and direct analytical tools for management. It provides insight into the relationship between revenue, costs, and net income.

The retail industry tracks break even on an annual basis. Break-even in retail doesn't usually occur until late in November. That is why we call the Friday after Thanksgiving Black Friday. That is when most retail operations go from operating in the "red" (at a loss) to operating in the "black" (making a profit). Red and black refer to the ink colors used in accounting ledgers to denote a loss or a profit.

Target Income Sales

The break-even point relates to the concept of **Target Income Sales**.

Target Income Sales is the required revenue to achieve a budgeted profit goal. A CEO may focus on a target net income (profit) number. This goal needs translation into a sales revenue target for the sales team. Target Income Sales is a way of backing out the sales required to achieve a profit goal.

The calculation is similar to breakeven analysis. Here is the formula:

(Fixed costs + Target income) ÷ Contribution margin percentage

Lets say a company's president wants to achieve profits of $1,000,000. The firm's fixed costs are $2,400,000 and the average contribution margin percentage (revenue minus variable costs) is 40%. In this case Target Income Sales is $8,500,00:

($2,400,000 Fixed costs plus $1,000,000 Target income)/40% Contribution margin percentage = $8,500,000

The Target Income represents the desired income point. Target Income Sales are the sales targets developed in the budget.

Cost-Volume-Profit Analysis

Cost–volume–profit (CVP) is an analytic tool based on cost accounting measures. CVP analysis is a framework for figuring out how you get to profitability. It can be very useful for making decisions and analysis.

CVP analysis expands on **break-even** analysis. An important transition point in CVP analysis is the break-even. This is where total revenues equal total costs. At **break-even** an enterprise has no profit or loss and costs are covered.

CVP is based on the same assumptions as break-even analysis:

- Costs and revenues behave linearly.
- Costs are either fixed or variable.
- The amount of activity is the only factor affecting costs.
- All the units produced are sold. There is no inventory build up.
- The product mix remains constant.

The CVP elements are:

- Activity Level
- Unit prices
- Unit Variable Cost
- Total fixed costs

Economics is considered a science. Science seeks to gain insights by using assumptions to reduce complexity. Managerial economics reduces the complexity of situations to gain better understanding and insight. This insight is helpful for informed decision making and future planning.

CVP assumptions create a simplified linear model of how costs and profits interact. This interaction plots levels of volume sold at a consistent unit price. Increases in volume effect total revenues and costs in a linear fashion. This is because we assume constant costs and prices.

CVP identifies the contribution of revenue to cover fixed costs. This **contribution margin** is what is left after variable costs are covered. The nature of the **contribution margin** is the main insight of CVP. If the unit price is greater than the unit variable cost, then each successive unit sold will chip away at fixed costs. The break-even point is a special case of CVP where revenue covers total fixed and variable costs.

The following are the formulas for deriving CVP:

Total Costs = Total Fixed Costs + (unit variable costs X number of units)

Total Revenues = Sales Price X number of units

Now we need a little algebra. Don't be intimidated. We are just putting the elements of the above formulas into abbreviations:

$TC = FC + V \times U$

$TR = P \times U$

Where:

- TC = Total costs
- FC = Total fixed costs
- V = Unit variable cost
- U = Number of units
- TR = Total revenue or Sales

- P = Sales price per unit

We calculate profit as TR-TC. It is a profit if this is a positive number and a loss if it is negative.

Next we unbundle the components of Costs and Sales. This will provide further insight into operations. We will do this by deriving a formula for the contribution margin. This will take a bit more algebraic manipulation. Hang with me and don't let the algebra intimidate you. It will follow the narrative description above about what the Contribution Margin means.

First, we separate total costs into the fixed and variable costs components:

TC = FC + V x U

We can now unbundle the components of sales as **contribution** plus variable costs. **Contribution** is what's left after deducting variable costs from sales. Before achieving break-even, contribution goes towards offsetting fixed costs. After breakeven, contribution is the amount of a unit sale going towards profit.

$$TR = C \times U + V \times U$$

We can think of profit/loss (PL) as the contribution margin from the units sold minus the total fixed costs:

$$PL = C \times U - TFC$$

CVP analysis is a framework for figuring out how you get to profitability. It describes how many units at what price you need to sell to cover all your costs. In practice, the assumptions can limit its accuracy. It is a way to get a handle on the dynamics of how your cost structure affects your goal of turning a profit. And turning a profit is how you remain a sustainable business.

Cost Accounting Summary

Cost accounting is a fundamental set of tools for analyzing a business and making decisions. Cost accounting overlaps with finance in making informed managerial decisions. Now that you are familiar with cost accounting terminology and techniques, put them to use ASAP!

Tax Accounting

Tax accounting is also its own specialty and profession. The rules differ from state to state in the U.S. and tax laws and rules change on a regular basis. Keeping up with these changes and their implications is a full time job. Tax accounting in the US is governed by the Internal Revenue Code and overseen by the Internal Revenue Service (IRS) which dictates the specific rules that companies and individuals must follow when preparing their tax returns. Tax accounting principles differ from Generally Accepted Accounting Principles (GAAP).

There are several taxing authorities that you need to be aware of and remain in compliance with: Federal (IRS), and State and local authorities, such as county or city. Hire the services of a CPA that specializes in taxes to help you initially prepare and file quarterly estimates and tax returns.

Never defer paying taxes and contemplate using the tax money to finance the business. You may rationalize that you only need it to cover expenses for a short while and then will pay the taxes later. This is a slippery slope and a recipe for disaster; do not fall into this trap.

Summary

The Foundational Importance and Impact of Accounting in Modern Life

The history of accounting is several thousand of years old and can be traced back to the great ancient civilizations. The early development of accounting dates back to ancient Mesopotamia and the Sumerians, and is closely related to the basic developments of writing, counting and money. The Egyptians and Babylonians had developed extensive auditing and accounting systems. By the time of the Emperor Augustus two thousand years ago, the Roman government had access to detailed financial information relating to their empire.

The invention of double entry bookkeeping is attributed to Luca Pacioli. He was a Franciscan monk and is referred to as the father of accounting. The book in which he describes double entry bookkeeping was a mathematics text called the *Summa de Arithmetica, Geometria, Proportioni et Proportionalita.* He wrote it in 1494. Luca was living with Leonardo da Vinci at the time in Milan and was Leonardo's math tutor.

The first actual recorded description of double entry bookkeeping was in 1458 in a work titled: *Book on the Art of Trade.* The author's name was Benedikt Kotruljević. He was born in Dubrovnik in 1416.

Double entry bookkeeping is one of the great intellectual breakthroughs and turning points in history. It is the basis of modern accounting. This method enables traders, merchants, entrepreneurs, to accurately keep track of every transaction in detail. It provides investors with an accurate summary of the business activities of an enterprise.

Accounting allows people to organize massive amounts of transactional information and produce summary financial statements. These financial statements distill the information into readable form that communicates the operational performance of a business.

The income statement shows total revenues minus total expenses, leaving either a profit or loss. The balance sheet illustrates the assets, the debts, and the difference between them as owners' equity.

These financial tools have enabled business owners, investors, and governments to allocate resources more effectively. For example, if a business person owned two shops, they could look at each income statement and review the profits or loss. From this information they are able to determine in which one to invest more money, effort and time; or which one to close.

As this type of analysis developed, more decisions began to be made using the information provided by accounting. This led to more efficient and effective use and deployment of capital. Capital grew, and as it did so did the surplus benefits to society.

From analysis of the income statement the idea of the return on investment (ROI) evolved. ROI enabled investors to compare investments objectively with the simple ratio formula. They could then double down on the better performing ones.

Investors, bankers, and the business community started to add calculations and assessments of risk to the analysis. An entrepreneur might ask: if we could make a $1,000 on investment A and a $1,000 on investment B, which one has the least risk thereby making the investment safer? Or which investment has the more important outcome, making bearing the risk more acceptable? This combination of risk and return into business analysis became the basis of Corporate Finance.

Organizing financial information and the results of operations into the balance sheet has had a great impact as well. The balance sheet shows how assets are financed and grow by reducing accounting into a simple elegant equation: Assets = Liabilities + Owners' Equity. The equation shows that everything owned is financed with a combination of debt and equity.

With these insights owners, investors and entrepreneurs were able to value their assets more accurately and to sell them to others for what they were worth. People began to make better and wiser decisions and became financially literate. This drove markets to develop around the world. Wealth has been created on an unprecedented scale, lifting millions of people out of poverty. Accounting is foundational in the modern capitalist economic miracle.

Next Steps

In this book we have gone over bookkeeping; financial statement preparation and basic analysis; budgeting and financial projections.

Accounting is not a spectator sport. You will really learn accounting by doing it. But first you need to know what to do. Jump-starting through the complexity of that paradox is no small feat.

Your intention to learn is the first step. Purchasing this book was the second step. Journeys start with initial steps. But they are of no use to you unless you read it, comprehend the ideas and internalize the concepts. As you are reading this: Congratulations! You have digested the material. No one can take that away from you. This is an accomplishment that you can be proud of.

Now that you have read through it once, you may want to return to sections again more thoughtfully until you own this subject.

Now you are part of this tradition. It's now time to put your accounting knowledge to work! Go forth and prosper!

This leads to our next related topic: Finance. Check out MBA ASAP Guide to Corporate Finance. It is an award winning book on the subject.

Accounting Concepts, Principals, and Glossary

Accounting Principals

Accountants often need to make judgments. We make decisions relative to recording and presenting transactions in the clearest and most meaningful way. We use consistent principles to guide our decision-making process. Here are some general rules and concepts.

- **Matching principle:** This principle states that a company's revenue should be matched with the expenses that relate to that revenue. The concept of simultaneously recognizing the revenues and expenses that jointly result from the same transactions.

- **Principle of conservatism:** Conservatism relates to decisions about presentation and reporting. Reporting should err on the side of generating the least attractive financial result. If there's a decision about revenue, the conservative choice is to delay recognizing revenue in the financial statements. Expenses should be posted to the financial statements sooner rather than later. These choices generate financial statements that are less optimistic and less likely to mislead investors and potential investors. The idea is to manage expectations and not mislead investors and other parties that make decisions about the financial viability of the company based on the presentation in the financial statements.

- **Materiality:** refers to the judgment standard of what level of detail is significant to report on financial statements. It is about relevancy and importance. The concept that accounting should disclose separately only those events that are relatively important. Materiality defines the threshold at which financial information becomes relevant to the decision making needs of users. Information is deemed material if its omission or misstatement could influence the economic decisions of users. Accounting information is deemed material if the judgment of a reasonable person relying on the information would have been changed or influenced by the omission or misstatement. Materiality relates to the significance of transactions and is relative to the size and circumstances of individual companies and situations.

- **Fair value accounting** is a financial reporting approach in which companies are permitted to revalue certain assets and liabilities based on estimates of the current prices. Because historical prices can be misleading, companies make estimates of what they currently would receive if they were to sell the assets or would pay if they were to be purchased. An active market or other objective basis of valuation is very important in this regard.

- **True and Fair View of Financial Statements** are auditing and financial reporting concepts. True and fair view in auditing means that the financial statements are free from material misstatements and faithfully represent the financial performance and position of the company. **True** means that the financial statements are factually correct and have been prepared according to GAAP in the US or IFRS for international companies. They do not contain any material misstatements that may mislead users. **Fair** means the financial statements present the information faithfully without any bias and that they substantially reflect the economic transactions being reported.

Common Accounting Terms Glossary

These are important words and phrases, in alphabetical order, you will become familiar with as you study and acquire a working knowledge of accounting:

Account

An account is a device for accumulating additions and subtractions relating to a single asset, liability, or owner's equity item, including revenues and expenses. An account is a record used to classify the transaction activity that is recorded in the General Ledger.

Account balance

An account balance is the sum of debit entries minus the sum of credit entries in an account. If positive, the difference is called a debit balance; if negative, a credit balance.

Accounting

Accounting is a service activity whose function is to provide quantitative information, primarily financial in nature, about economic entities that is intended to be useful in making economic decisions. Accounting is the recording and reporting of financial transactions, including the origination of the transaction, its recognition, processing, and summarization in the financial statements.

Accounts Payable

Accounts Payable is an amount owed *by* the enterprise for delivered goods or completed services. Accounts Payable is a liability representing an amount owed to a creditor. In most companies checks are cut in batches and obligations are first entered through Accounts Payable accounts before they are paid. It is normally a current liability.

Accounts Receivable

Account Receivable is an amount owed *to* the enterprise from a completed sales transaction or for services rendered. Accounts Receivable is an asset related to sales revenue. It is a claim against a debtor arising from sales or services rendered. Normally, a current asset.

Accrual Basis

Accrual basis is a method of accounting that recognizes revenue when earned, rather than when collected and expenses when incurred rather than when paid. It is the method of recognizing revenues as goods are sold (or delivered) and as services are rendered, independent of the time when case is received. Expenses are recognized in the period when the related revenue is recognized independent of the time when cash is paid out. Accrual basis creates an accurate picture of transactions. Enterprises use the accrual basis for their accounting as opposed to a cash basis. Accrual accounting is a consequence of implementing the Matching Principle.

Additional Paid-in Capital (APIC)

The Additional Paid-in Capital (APIC) account is where the amount paid for a share of stock, less the par value, is recorded. Another alternative title for the account is *capital contributed in excess of par value*.

Adjusting Entries

Adjusting entries are journal entries usually made at the end of an accounting period to allocate income and expenditures to the period in which they actually occurred. It is an entry made at the end of an accounting period to record a transaction or other accounting event, which for some reason has not been recorded or has been improperly recorded during the accounting period. It is an entry to update the accounts.

Adjusted Trial Balance

An adjusted trial balance is a listing of all the account titles and balances contained in the general ledger after the adjusting entries for an accounting period have been posted to the accounts. The adjusted trial balance is an internal document. It is not a financial statement but is used to create the financial statements.

Amortization

Amortization is the process of liquidating or extinguishing a debt with a series of payments to creditor. It refers to the calculation and schedule of the paying off of debt with fixed repayments in regular installments over a period of time. Consumers are most likely to encounter amortization with a mortgage or car loan. Amortization can mean the accounting for the payments themselves. An amortization schedule for a mortgage is a table showing the allocation between interest and principle.

Amortization can also mean the spreading out of capital expenses for intangible assets over a specific period of time (usually over the asset's useful life) for accounting and tax purposes. Amortization is similar to depreciation, which is used for tangible assets, and to depletion, which is used with natural resources. Amortization roughly matches an asset's expense with the revenue it generates.

Asset

An asset is what the enterprise owns. An asset is defined as having probable future economic benefits obtained or controlled by an entity as a result of past transactions. For example: land, factories, office buildings, equipment, vehicles, cash in bank accounts, other investments, accounts receivable, and intellectual property such as patents and trademarks.

Audit

An audit is a systematic inspection of accounting records involving analyses, tests, and confirmations. It is a formal examination and official endorsement of the accuracy of the financial statements of the enterprise conducted by an independent certified public accountant

(CPA). In the U.S., an audit is based on GAAP and FASB rules. Most companies are required to have an audit performed each fiscal year.

Balance Sheet

A Balance Sheet is a summary report of a company's financial position on a specific date that shows Total Assets = Total Liabilities + Owner's Equity.

Bookkeeping

Bookkeeping is the process of analyzing and recording of financial transactions in the accounting records. Transactions include purchases, sales, receipts and payments by an individual or organization.

The Books

The "books" is a general term referring to the General Ledger and the various journals that are kept by a business. *Book* can be used as a verb: to record a transaction.

Book Value

Book value is the value of an asset according to its balance sheet account balance. For assets, the value is based on the original cost of the asset less any depreciation, amortization or impairment costs made against the asset. It refers to the net amount.

Budget

A budget is a financial plan that is used to estimate the results of future operations. A budget is an estimate of revenue and expense activity for a fiscal year or period. It is used to help control future operations. A budget can be created for a department or a project. In a corporation, budgets are aggregated up to the corporate level and reviewed and approved by the board of directors. The budget then becomes an operational document for the coming year and actual results are measured against it. In governmental operations, budgets often become the law.

Capitalize

To capitalize is to record an expenditure that will benefit a future period as an asset rather than to treat it as an expense in the period of its occurrence. It is an accounting method used to delay the recognition of a significant expense by recording the expense as a long-term asset. In general, capitalizing expenses more accurately depicts the situation as companies acquiring new assets with a long-term lifespan can spread out the cost over a specified period of time. That period of time is an estimate of the asset's useful life, when it will be contributing to the generation of revenues.

Cash

Cash is currency and coins, negotiable checks, and balances in bank accounts. We all know what cash is but in accounting it refers to the first account in the Assets category of the Balance Sheet. This is aggregated from all company bank accounts and it is derived as the bottom number on the Cash Flow Statement.

Cash Flow Statement

A cash flow statement is a financial statement that shows how changes in balance sheet accounts and income affect cash. The cash flow statement breaks the analysis down into operating, investing and financing activities.

Chart of Accounts

The chart of accounts is a listing of all accounts used in the **general ledger** of an organization. The chart is used by the accounting software to aggregate information into an entity's financial statements. It is a list of the names and numbers, systematically organized, of accounts.

Common Stock

Common Stock is the type of stock that is present in every corporation. Shares of common stock provide evidence of ownership in a corporation. These shares represent the class of owners who have residual claims on the assets and earnings of a corporation after all debt and preferred shareholders' claims have been met. Holders of common stock elect the corporation's directors and share in the distribution of profits of the company via dividends. If the corporation were to liquidate, the secured lenders would be paid first, followed by unsecured lenders, preferred stockholders (if any), and lastly the common stockholders. If a company is acquired, the proceeds go to the shareholders after the debts are paid off.

Cost of Goods Sold

Cost of Goods Sold (COGS) is the direct costs attributable to the production of the goods sold by a company. This amount includes the cost of the materials used in creating the good along with the direct labor costs used to produce the good. It *excludes* indirect expenses such as distribution costs, marketing and sales force costs.

Credit

A credit is an entry on the right side of a double-entry accounting system that represents the reduction of an asset or expense or the addition to a liability or revenue. It is the countervailing entry to a debit.

Current Assets

Current Assets are balance sheet accounts that represent the value of assets that are reasonably expected to be converted into cash within one year in the normal course of business. Current assets include cash, accounts receivable, inventory, marketable securities, prepaid expenses and other liquid assets that can be readily converted to cash.

Debit

A debit is an entry on the left side of a double-entry accounting system that represents the addition to an asset or expense or the reduction to a liability or revenue. It is the countervailing entry to a credit.

Debt

Debt is an amount owed usually for funds borrowed. Debt is the general name for loans, notes, bonds, mortgages, and the like that are evidence of amounts owed and have definite payment dates and schedules. The lender agrees to lend funds to the borrower upon a promise by the borrower to pay interest on the debt, usually with the interest to be paid at regular intervals. Debt is a Liability to the company (an asset to the lender) and is shown on the balance sheet net of how much has been repaid.

Depreciation

Depreciation is a method of allocating the cost of a tangible asset over its useful life. It is the process of allocating the cost of an asset to the periods of benefit. Businesses depreciate long-term assets for both tax and accounting purposes. Different depreciation schedules are used for different fixed assets. Depreciation schedules can vary in length and also in how fast depreciation is incurred. There are accelerated depreciation techniques that apply more depreciation to early years in the schedule. Depreciation can also mean a decrease in an asset's value caused by unfavorable market conditions.

Dividend

A dividend is a payment made by a **corporation** to its **shareholders**, usually as a distribution of a portion of **profits**. When a corporation earns a profit or surplus, it can re-invest it in the business (called **retained earnings**), and/or pay a fraction of the profit as a dividend to shareholders. A dividend can be paid in cash (cash dividend) or stock (stock dividend).

Double-Entry Accounting

Double entry is the system of recording transactions that maintains the equality of the accounting equation. Each entry results in recording equal amounts of debits and credits. Double-entry accounting is a method of recording financial transactions in which each transaction is entered in two or more accounts and involves two-way, self-balancing posting. Total debits must equal total credits.

Equity

Equity is a claim on assets. Equity is short for owner's equity or shareholder's equity. It consists of the net assets of an enterprise. It is the residual interest in the assets of an entity that remains after deducting its liabilities. Net assets are the difference between the total assets of the entity and all its liabilities. Equity appears on the balance sheet. Remember the balance sheet formula: Assets = Liabilities + Equity.

Expense

An expense is funds paid by the enterprise. For example: paychecks to employees, and payments to vendors for goods or services. It is a decrease in owners' equity caused by the using up of assets in producing revenue or carrying out other activities that are part of the entity's operations.

FASB

FASB stands for Financial Accounting Standards Board and is an independent, private, nongovernmental authority for the establishment of *generally accepted accounting principles* in the United States.

Financial Statements

Financial Statements are a series of reports showing a summary view of the various financial activities of a company. There are three major financial statements: Balance Sheet, Income Statement, and Cash Flow Statement. Each statement tells a different story about the financial activity of an enterprise. Financial statements also include the notes thereto.

Fiscal Year

A fiscal year is a period of 12 consecutive months chosen by a business as its accounting period for annual reports. Most fiscal years are a calendar year (January 1-December 31) but a fiscal year can start and end on any month. For example most government agencies run a fiscal year from October 1 – September 30.

Fixed Asset

A fixed asset is any tangible item with a useful life of more than one year, for example-office buildings, factories, major equipment and vehicles. Computers used to be thought of as fixed assets but personal computers now cost less than $1,000 and have useful lives of not much more than a year and so are usually expensed instead of capitalized as a fixed asset. A fixed asset is an asset and is listed on the Balance Sheet.

GAAP

GAAP stands for Generally Accepted Accounting Principles which are conventions, rules, and procedures that are required to be followed in preparing financial statements. GAAP defines accepted accounting practice in the U.S. These principles are defined by FASB. They include both broad guidelines and detailed practices and procedures.

General Ledger

The general ledger is the collection of all the financial statement accounts including: asset, liability, equity, revenue and expense accounts. The general ledger is what is used to prepare financial statements.

Income Statement

An Income Statement is a summary report that shows revenues, expenses, gains or losses over a specific period of time, typically a month, quarter or fiscal year. An income statement is structured as: Revenue – Expenses = Net Income. Net Income is also referred to as Profit or Earnings. The *earnings-per-share* amount is usually shown on the income statement.

Intellectual Property

Intellectual Property (IP) is a broad categorical description for the set of intangibles owned and legally protected by a company from outside use or implementation without consent. From an accounting standpoint, Intellectual property can consist of patents, copyrights, and trademarks. IP are assets listed on the balance sheet and valued at the cost of procuring them net of depreciation.

Journal Entry

A journal entry is a group of debit and credit transactions that are posted to the general ledger. All journal entries must net to zero so debits must equal credits. An explanation of the transaction is included, if necessary.

Leverage

Operating leverage refers to the tendency of net income to rise at a faster rate than sales when there are fixed costs. Financial leverage means the use of long-term debt in securing funds for the enterprise. A measure of financial leverage is the debt to equity ratio. It is calculated as the ratio of a company's loan capital (debt) to the value of its common stock (equity). Debt/Equity.

Liability

A liability is an obligation to pay a definite amount at a definite time in return for a past or current benefit. It is what the company owes. For example: loans, taxes, payables, long term debt from a bond issue.

Line of Credit (LOC)

A line of credit is an arrangement between a financial institution, usually a bank, and a customer for short term borrowings on demand. The borrower can draw down on the line of credit at any time, but cannot exceed the maximum   set   in   the   agreement.

Liquidity

Liquidity refers to the availability of cash, or near cash resources, for meeting a firm's obligations.

Mark-to-market

Mark-to-market or fair value accounting refers to accounting for the "fair value" of an asset or liability based on the current market price, or for similar assets and liabilities, or based on another objectively assessed "fair" value. Fair value accounting has been a part of Generally Accepted Accounting Principles (GAAP) in the United States since the early 1990s.

Net Income (loss)

Net Income (loss) is the amount the company made or lost for a specific period of time. It is the excess of all revenues and gains for a period over all expenses and losses of the period. It is the bottom number on the Income Statement. To arrive at net income take total revenues minus total expenses. Net Income is sometimes called Profit or Earnings.

P & L responsibility

P&L stands for profit and loss statement or income statement. P & L responsibility is one of the most important responsibilities of any executive position. It involves monitoring, and being judged on, the net income after expenses for a department or entire organization. The executive's performance is judged on the financial results. The executive has direct influence on how company resources are allocated and how tactics are developed to implement strategy.

Par Value

Par value is the face amount of a security. The Par Value account is a stock equity account shown on the Balance Sheet. It is a way to keep track of the amount of shares outstanding. The par value is a small monetary value attributed to each share. It is an arbitrary number, usually $.01

Preferred Stock

Preferred Stock is a class of corporation stock with claims to income or assets after bondholders but before common shares. Preferred stock provides for preferential treatment of dividends. Preferred stockholders will be paid dividends before the common stockholders receive dividends. These dividends are sometimes paid in stock instead of money.

Principal

Principal refers to the face amount of a loan. It is the original sum invested or lent.

Retained Earnings

The percentage of net income not paid out as dividends, but *retained* by the company to be reinvested in its core business, or to pay debt. It is recorded under shareholders' equity on the balance sheet and is measured as owners' equity less contributed capital.

Revenue

Revenue is funds collected by the company usually from sales. It is the monetary measure of sales or services rendered.

SEC

Securities and Exchange Commission, the agency authorized by the U.S. Congress to regulate, among other things, the financial reporting practices of public corporations.

Shares Outstanding

A company's stock currently held by all its shareholders, including restricted shares owned by the company's officers and insiders. Outstanding shares are shown on a company's balance sheet under the heading "Capital Stock." The number of outstanding shares is used in calculating key metrics such as a company's market capitalization, as well as its earnings per share (EPS).

Stock

Stock, or shares, is the general term used to describe the ownership certificates of a company. Stocks are the investment instrument or vehicle of equity.

T-accounts

A T-account is an account from shaped like the letter T with the title above the horizontal line. Debits are shown to the left of the vertical line and credits to the right. Accountants and bookkeepers often use T-accounts as a graphical aid for visualizing and understanding the effect of the debit and credit on the two (or more) accounts related to a journal entry.

Trial Balance

A trial balance is a listing of account balances. All accounts with debit balances are totaled separately from accounts with credit balances. The two totals should be equal. Trial balances are taken as a partial check of the arithmetic accuracy of the entries previously made.

A company prepares a trial balance periodically, usually at the end of every reporting period, as the initial step in preparing financial statements. This statement of all debits and credits is used to quickly locate any disagreements indicating an error. The trial balance is a trouble shooting tool.

Vendor List

The vendor list shows information about the people or companies from whom an enterprise buys goods and services, including banks and tax agencies.

The End

Thank you for reading!

Dear Reader,

I hope you enjoyed **MBA ASAP Learn Accounting Fast!** and found it filled with useful and valuable information..

As an author, I love feedback. Candidly, you are the reason that I organize my thoughts, write, and explore these topics. So, tell me what you liked, what was helpful and what could be better explained or left out. You can write me at jjcousins@gmail.com and visit me on the web at www.mba-asap.com.

Finally, I need to ask a favor. If you were so inclined, I'd love a review on Amazon. I'd really appreciate your feedback.

Reviews can be tough to come by these days. You, the reader, have the power now to make or break a book. A quick review will be immensely appreciated!

Thank you so much for reading and for spending the time and effort with me.

In deep gratitude,

John Cousins

Sign up for my Newsletter and get free books. Sign up at www.mba-asap.com and receive Reading and Understanding Financial Statements absolutely free.

Receive announcements of free and discounted books and courses.

About the Author

John is an author of over 20 books, blogger, podcaster, online course creator, investor, inventor, entrepreneur and musician. John began his career, after graduating from Boston University and MIT with degrees in Media Studies and Electronics, working for one of the great early Silicon Valley tech firms: Ampex. He then spent a decade in Manhattan working for ABC Television as a systems engineer designing and building facilities for the network and managing programs for sports and news; big spectacles like the Olympics and political conventions.

John then received his MBA from Wharton. He has since taken two companies public as CFO and CEO and has had 15 years experience as a public company CFO and ten years experience as a public company CEO. John has been involved in many start up and public company financings and deal making. He has founded numerous startups in alternative energy, life sciences, and technology. His career shifted to teaching at numerous universities in US and internationally in the past ten years. His company MBA ASAP delivers digital content on business topics via eBooks, paperbacks, audiobooks, podcasts and online courses. Visit www.mba-asap.com

FREE EBOOK
DOWNLOADS

Go to www.mba-asap.com and click on the big orange button

www.ingramcontent.com/pod-product-compliance
Lightning Source LLC
Chambersburg PA
CBHW070240190526
45169CB00001B/240